MAP CASE

100
Topographic Maps

illustrating physiographic features

100
Topographic Maps

Text by Richard DeBruin

illustrating physiographic features

Consultant:

W. Hilton Johnson

Department of Geology

University of Illinois, Urbana

Maps reproduced
from "*A Set of
100 Topographic Maps
Illustrating Specified
Physiographic Features,*"
created by the
U.S. Geological
Survey, Department of
the Interior,
Washington, D.C.

 **Hubbard Press**
A division of Hubbard Scientific Company

Book design by Don Walkoe

Copyright © 1970, Hubbard Scientific
Company. All rights reserved.
No part of this book may be reproduced
in any form without written permission
from the publisher: Hubbard Press,
Hubbard Scientific Company, 2855 Shermer Road,
Northbrook, Illinois, 60062.

Printed in the United States of America

Contents

Introduction

100 Topographic Maps represents a condensation, indeed a distillation of the superb compilation of quadrangle maps created by the United States Department of the Interior Geological Survey. The book depicts in striking form major physiographic features of the continental United States in a collection appropriate for earth science and geography studies, as well as specialized work in social studies, geology and topography.

Maps tell a shorthand story of the earth rendered in symbols, abstract representations and figures. Contour intervals illustrate dimension. Coded color adds further realism.

For the student of earth science or geology, there is both historical and current information on major landform features: a lacustrine plain, a Pleistocene shoreline, the San Andrea rift. The social scientist can be witness to the impact of man upon the land, the earth's cultural geography: tanks for watering stock, coal mining areas, oil fields. The political scientist will find international and state boundaries, built-up urban areas, place names, and indications of the not-so-subtle influence of topography upon the political affairs of man. The wealth of detail also enables the study of cultural hydrographic features: artificial lakes, reservoirs, levees and other flood control provisions, windmills, wells, locks and dams.

The topographic features are keyed to each map in a dual way: by legend or caption underneath the map and by a more detailed and extensive Index listing. Extraneous or peripheral details have been cropped out of the original quadrangles.

Each map is introduced with a description of its highlights, attention being given to both overall conformity of features as well as identification of exceptional physical and occasionally cultural aspects. Wherever possible, the legends which accompany each map are organized so as to consolidate and show patterns or continuity. For example, regions which exhibit both mountainous and alpine glaciation features in combination are often noted in the map legends. Drainage characteristics which are interrelated or affected by a common physiographic phenomenon may also be listed together in the map legend. Occasionally, as in strongly dissected mountainous areas of relatively older geologic age, even erosional results may be grouped in the legend.

For large-scale study, transfer or specialized research, each map legend contains in addition to scale and contour interval, the approximate latitudinal and longitudinal coordinates of the map inset. This grid is a constant for reference, establishing a framework for extension or contraction of research. An arbitrary grid is also provided on each map for convenient reference.

The various color plates, each adding its dimension to the USGS maps, should be noted for their particular and specialized contribution to the cartographic detail of the individual map. One of the primary functions of the brown plate, for instance, is to provide contour markings. Some of the maps contain a brown overlay tint to graphically illustrate the relief and dimension of particularly striking land features. The black plate symbols are largely confined to depicting cultural features, and of course, for type labels throughout the maps. Blue is the internationally recognized color for showing bodies of water (light blue), drainage (dark blue), as well as other varied hydrographic features.

The Indexes

The first index for *100 Topographic Maps* contains an alphabetically arranged list of maps by state, with physiographic features of the map inset itemized alphabetically under each index entry. For all maps it would be well for the student to compare the more detailed index entry against the individual map legend to determine any additional details which may be found on the map. The second index is an alphabetical listing of physiographic features under 12 major headings; each feature is identified by individual map and page number. The 12 major headings are: Coastal Features and Shorelines, Escarpment Features, Glaciation Features (Alpine), Glaciation Features (Continental), Miscellaneous Features, Mountain Features, Plains Features, Plateau Features, Solution Features, Valley Features, Volcanic Features, Water Features, and Wind Features. Included in the *miscellaneous* category are such relatively rare or occasional phenomena as divides, natural bridges, highest peaks, etc.

Landforms and Topography

Any highly selective compilation of maps such as this can, with study, lead to some striking general observations. For instance, the enormous impact of the geologic Ice Ages and continental glaciation upon almost the entire northern third of the conterminous United States can be vividly seen in these maps. The massive scouring; the alteration, interruption, re-routing and burial of ancient drainage systems; the deposits of transplanted rocks, tillage, and soil; the creation of new drainage systems, of lakes and rivers—all can be visualized in terms of the enormous lengths of time and the profound working of natural forces that have brought them about. Alpine glaciation, by contrast, while exhibiting certain exceptional features, does not have the awesome conglomerate effect of the moraines, drumlins, kames, kettles and glacial lakes that dominate the gigantic continental glaciation landscape.

Some individual maps exhibit a wide variety of topographic features while others illustrate a concentrated view of specific and related features.

Such maps as Crater Lake, Oregon, or Point Reyes, California, respectively have a generous amount of volcanic and coastal features; enough to challenge the student into cataloging, examining cause and effect, and exploring the unique combination of circumstances that produced these specific landforms in these precise locations. Monadnock, New Hampshire, which gave its name to the isolated glacial hill in an otherwise featureless peneplain, is a good introduction to an investigation of the evidence and effects of continental glaciation. Mount Tom, California, on the other hand, is an arena representing many of the major aspects of alpine glaciation, including arêtes, cirques, cirque lakes and cols.

Juanita Arch, Colorado is a good illustration of

escarpments; the inset of the Lake McBride, Kansas map is an introduction to plains features; mountain features are more widely scattered, but the Waldron, Arkansas with its folded mountains, ridges, hogbacks and knobs is a good place to start. Still other maps such as Lansford, North Dakota (with its 10-foot contour interval) shows a degree of surface uniformity that is a salient characteristic of many other large areas of our country.

Wind and water are the natural phenomena that have literally shaped the land and left features of a broad variety. The effects of wind and cumulative weathering can be seen in the regions of shifting sand dunes and hills—and strikingly in the buried lumber town of Singapore on the Kalamazoo River (Fennville, Michigan map). Another map illustrating a rare combination of wind features is Ashby, Nebraska. Requiring more investigation, but also indicative of the erosional force of wind and weather, are the different maps in which plateaus and mountains are the prominent features, especially in arid regions of the country. It would be a mistake, however, to assume that all desert/mountain regions of the country will have dunes or that the effects of weathering are limited to such prominent features. Spectacular examples of the force of the wind can be seen in such areas of the country as the Dust Bowl of the 1930's in the Great Plains and the loess deposits in the north central United States.

Drainage patterns, though largely reflective of geologic age and the condition of underlying rock strata, are nevertheless important enough to justify prominent treatment in the *Index by Feature* (under Valley Features) and in the individual map legends. Dendritic, trellis, radial and rectangular drainage are readily observable patterns on a topographic map; not visible, however, are the causes of such drainage patterns. A dendritic or tree-like branching of streams and rivers is characteristic of regions in which there are hard or resistant underlying rock formations; trellis patterns form along parallel folded rock strata; radial drainage usually has its head or source in a hill or mountain; and rectangular patterns occur where right-angled joints and faults control the water flow and direction.

Drainage patterns, although they are evidence of the order, design and regularity in nature, are not, however, indicative of the great erosional and energy potentials of streams and rivers. Deltas (with or without distributary channels), flood plains, alluvial fans and natural levees are among the more striking results of the work of rivers. The map of Philipp, Mississippi is a good basic reference for a general survey of both the impact and the effects of water on the land. Meanders, such as those on the Mississippi Alluvial Plain at Philipp, can be studied in detail. The considerable variation of this physiographic feature is apparent on the maps: entrenched meanders, meander scars, meander flood plains, meander cores and spurs, and the cutoff meander which creates the interesting vestigial remnant of the old stream bed—the oxbow lake.

Stream or tributary piracy (capture), another geologic phenomenon can be observed in *100 Topographic Maps*. Rivers on weaker rock strata will erode headward or upstream faster than less "well-adjusted" or often smaller tributary streams on harder rock strata. The result, facilitated if the two streams have courses at angles to and in different directions from each other, can be stream capture of one by the better-adjusted stream. The more diffuse the drainage pattern or the greater the effect of glacial alterations, the more common the possibility of such piracy.

Cultural Features

Although these are topographic maps, the cultural "evidence" man has left upon the land is also apparent and reflects not only man's continuing effort to control his environment but also his successful attempts to reap nature's bounty and harness her energy. Adapting and controlling the environment has led to artificial canals, irrigation systems, flood control engineering and reservoirs. Man's efforts to control his environment are impressive, whether they are efforts to bring water to a parched earth through irrigation or an urbanization which has no boundaries and which "expands" into the natural environment. Reaping nature's bounty has led man to plumb its natural resources—quarrying, oil wells, coal mines, damming the waters—and there is evidence of all of these in *100 Topographic Maps*. The energy resources of the earth—water, oil and coal—can also be studied independently in terms of their representation on these maps.

Explanations of the causes of such phenomena as drainage patterns, braided streams, alluvial fans, etc., may give some background but will hardly show the awesome and uncontrolled effects of unleashed water. Flood control provisions—like those shown on the Alma, Wisconsin/Minnesota map, or the dam, reservoir and river development complex known as the Tennessee Valley Authority (partially shown on the Norris, Tennessee map)—are clearly required to harness the excesses of water in a cultural environment. Other provisions such as dikes, artificial levees, spillways and secondary outlets may also be effective, and are illustrated in this collection of maps.

Paradoxically, the residue from floods can be quite beneficial to man. Rich bottom lands and flood-plains in this country attest to the agricultural increment that soil-carrying rivers discharge. Scholars continue to be amazed by the accurate calendar of Nile flooding that the Egyptians possessed thousands of years ago. And elsewhere, too, the alluvium deposited by floods as well as the controlled and retained flood waters of rivers serve man well. It was in the flood plains of mighty river valleys that early civilizations began and thrived. Not too surprisingly, man learned to use water at a faster rate and in a more sophisticated way than the earth's other natural resources.

Conclusion

Even the casual student can wonder at the infinite variety of the United States, from the tired old mountains of the east to the rugged young giants of the west; the arid plateaus to the drenched and humid swamps and bayous; the "thin" air and snow of three-mile-high mountains to the oppressive heat of below-sea-level depressions; and from the Great Plains to the Rockies. Such a study can lead to an awareness of what a great natural laboratory the continental United States really is.

Some of the more unique or exceptional topographic phenomena have been briefly mentioned in this *Introduction*, not only to contribute a sense of enthusiasm and investigative curiosity to this kind of study, but also to suggest that the proportions are generous enough to invite many investigations.

Man's tenuous control of his environment, his imperfect understanding of the balance of nature (and his frequent disturbance of it), and his inadequate attempts to rejuvenate what has already been plundered are challenges of enormous consequence. In this still continuing struggle—for that is what it is—specialists of every persuasion: earth scientist, geologist, botanist, marine engineer, conservationist, biologist and social scientist, are needed. This book with its broad coverage and in-depth study of landforms and topography will hopefully provide an effective tool in the investigation, discovery and understanding of the physiographic and cultural face of our land.

Map Symbols

Hard surface, heavy duty road, four or more lanes . . . . . .

Hard surface, heavy duty road, two or three lanes . . . .

Hard surface, medium duty road, four or more lanes . . . .

Hard surface, medium duty road, two or three lanes . . . . .

Improved light duty road . . . .

Unimproved dirt road and trail . . . .

Dual highway, dividing strip 25 feet or less . . . .

Dual highway, dividing strip exceeding 25 feet . . . .

Road under construction . . . .

Railroad, single track and multiple track . . . .

Railroads in juxtaposition . . . .

Narrow gage, single track and multiple track . . . .

Railroad in street and carline . . . .

Bridge, road and railroad . . . .

Drawbridge, road and railroad . . . .

Footbridge . . . .

Tunnel, road and railroad . . . .

Overpass and underpass . . . . ,

Important small masonry or earth dam . . . .

Dam with lock . . . .

Dam with road . . . .

Canal with lock . . . .

Buildings (dwelling, place of employment, etc.) . . . .

School, church, and cemetery . . . .

Buildings (barn, warehouse, etc.) . . . .

Power transmission line . . . .

Telephone line, pipeline, etc. (labeled as to type) . . . .

Wells other than water (labeled as to type) . . . . o Oil . . . . . o Gas

Tanks; oil, water, etc. (labeled as to type) . . . . • • ● ⊘ Water

Located or landmark object; windmill . . . . o

Open pit, mine, or quarry; prospect . . . . :⤬ x

Shaft and tunnel entrance . . . . ◾ . . . . Y

Horizontal and vertical control station:

    Tablet, spirit level elevation . . . . BM △ 5653

    Other recoverable mark, spirit level elevation . . . . △ 5455

Horizontal control station: tablet, vertical angle elevation VABM △ 9519

    Any recoverable mark, vertical angle or checked elevation △3775

Vertical control station: tablet, spirit level elevation . . . . . BM ✕ 957

    Other recoverable mark, spirit level elevation . . . . ✕ 954

Checked spot elevation . . . . ✕4675

Unchecked spot elevation and water elevation . . . . ✕ 5657 870

Boundary, national . . . .

    State . . . .

    County, parish, municipio . . . .

    Civil township, precinct, town, barrio . . . .

    Incorporated city, village, town, hamlet . . . .

    Reservation, national or state . . . .

    Small park, cemetery, airport, etc . . . .

    Land grant . . . .

Township or range line, United States land survey . . . . . .

Township or range line, approximate location . . . .

Section line, United States land survey . . . .

Section line, approximate location . . . .

Township line, not United States land survey . . . : . . . . . .

Section line, not United States land survey . . . .

Section corner, found and indicated . . . . + ... :

Boundary monument: land grant and other . . . . ▫

United States mineral or location monument . . . . . . , ... ▲

Index contour . . . . | Intermediate contour . .

Supplementary contour | Depression contours . .

Fill . . . . | Cut . . . .

Levee . . . . | Levee with road . . . . .

Mine dump . . . . | Wash . . . .

Tailings . . . . | Tailings pond . . . .

Strip mine . . . . | Distorted surface . . . .

Sand area . . . . | Gravel beach . . . .

Perennial streams . . . . | Intermittent streams . .

Elevated aqueduct . . . . | Aqueduct tunnel . . . . .

Water well and spring . . ∘ . . . . ∾ | Disappearing stream . .

Small rapids . . . . | Small falls . . . .

Large rapids . . . . | Large falls . . . .

Intermittent lake . . . . | Dry lake . . . .

Foreshore flat . . . . . . | Rock or coral reef . . . .

Sounding, depth curve . | Piling or dolphin . . . . . ∘

Exposed wreck . . . . . . | Sunken wreck . . . . +++

Rock, bare or awash; dangerous to navigation . . . . ✳

Marsh (swamp) . . . . | Submerged marsh . . .

Inundation area . . . . | Mangrove . . . .

10

MOBILE, ALABAMA Physiographic features include an abandoned Pleistocene shoreline (south to north, left of center, approximately 30-foot elevation), dissected plain, drowned valleys, marine terrace, partially obstructed outlet (Dog River), and unwooded tidal marshes and swamps (Alligator Bayou, for example).

Scale	1:62,500
Contour Interval	10 ft.
Latitude	30° 32′ N
	to 30° 40′ N
Longitude	88° 3′ W
	to 88° 11′ W

½   0   4 MILES

1 5 0   1   2   3   4   5 KILOMETERS

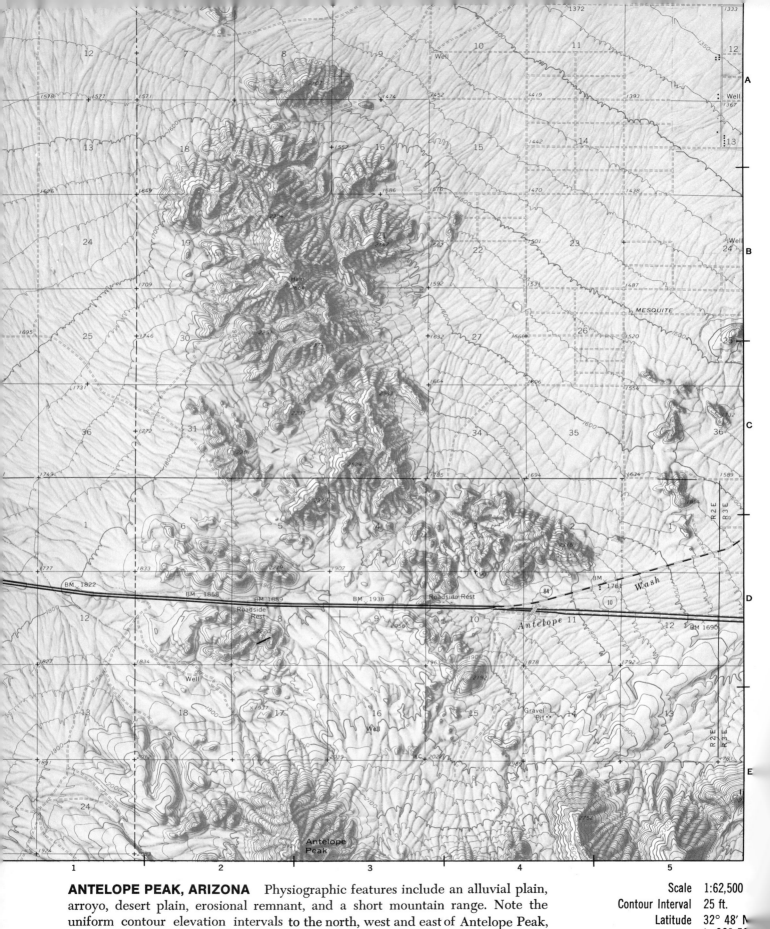

ANTELOPE PEAK, ARIZONA Physiographic features include an alluvial plain, arroyo, desert plain, erosional remnant, and a short mountain range. Note the uniform contour elevation intervals to the north, west and east of Antelope Peak, as well as the parallel drainage.

Scale 1:62,500
Contour Interval 25 ft.
Latitude 32° 48′ N
to 32° 56′
Longitude 112° 6′ W
to 112°

12

BRIGHT ANGEL, ARIZONA Physiographic features include a dissected plateau, points, cliffs with banded contouring, a fault-line valley (Bright Angel Canyon), rapids, rock terrace, Tonto Platform, and a V-shaped valley.

Scale 1:62,500

Contour Interval 80 ft.

Latitude 36° 3′ N
to 36° 12′ N

Longitude 112° 2′ W
to 112° 11′ W

13

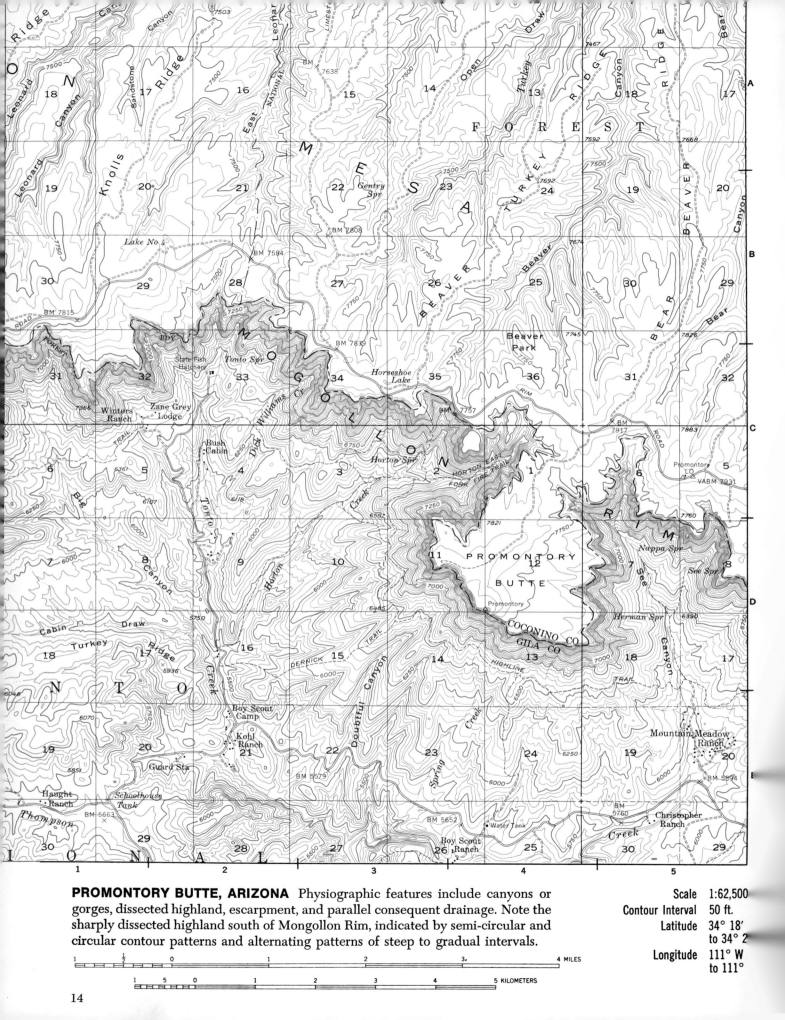

PROMONTORY BUTTE, ARIZONA Physiographic features include canyons or gorges, dissected highland, escarpment, and parallel consequent drainage. Note the sharply dissected highland south of Mongollon Rim, indicated by semi-circular and circular contour patterns and alternating patterns of steep to gradual intervals.

Scale 1:62,500
Contour Interval 50 ft.
Latitude 34° 18′ to 34° 2
Longitude 111° W to 111°

4 MILES

5 KILOMETERS

PAUL, ARKANSAS Physiographic features include a dissected plain, flood
plain, river bluff, and remnants of a plateau surface. Brannon Mountain and the
hills in the southwest sector of the map include the remnants of a plateau surface.

Scale 1:62,500
Contour Interval 20 ft.
Latitude 35° 46′ N
to 35° 54′ N
Longitude 93° 51′ W
to 93° 59′ W

½ 0 1 2 3 4 MILES

1 5 0 1 2 3 4 5 KILOMETERS

15

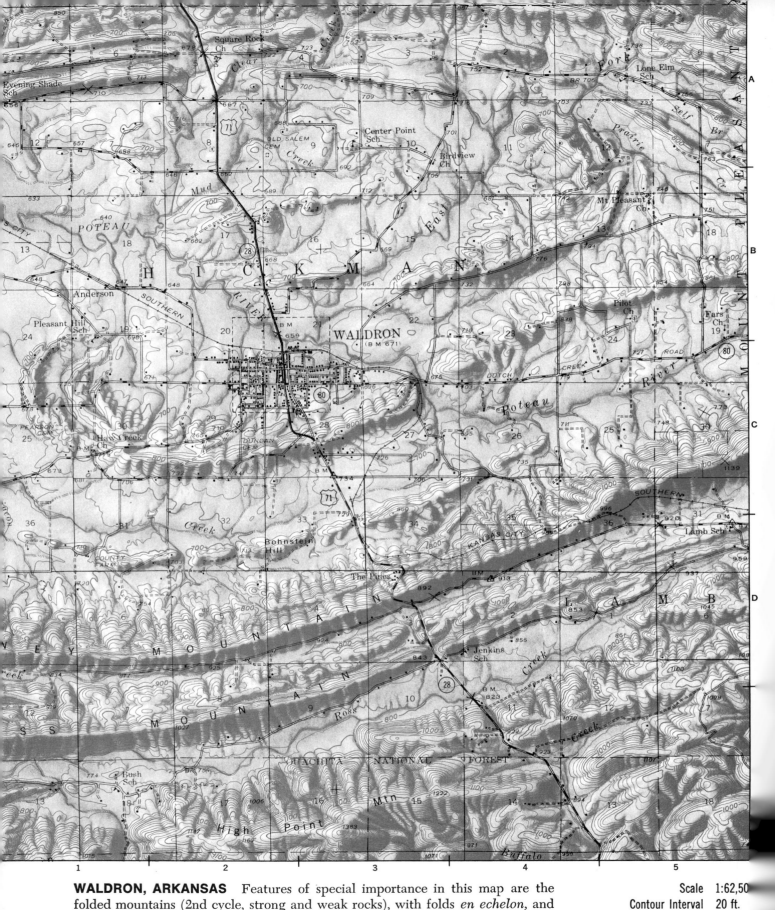

WALDRON, ARKANSAS Features of special importance in this map are the folded mountains (2nd cycle, strong and weak rocks), with folds *en echelon,* and hogbacks. Also note the knobs, the ridges formed of folded hard strata, strike ridges and valleys, and structurally controlled drainage (trellis type).

Scale 1:62,50
Contour Interval 20 ft.
Latitude 34° 49
to 34°
Longitude 94° 0'
to 94°

1 ½ 0 1 2 3 4 MILES

1 5 0 1 2 3 4 5 KILOMETERS

16

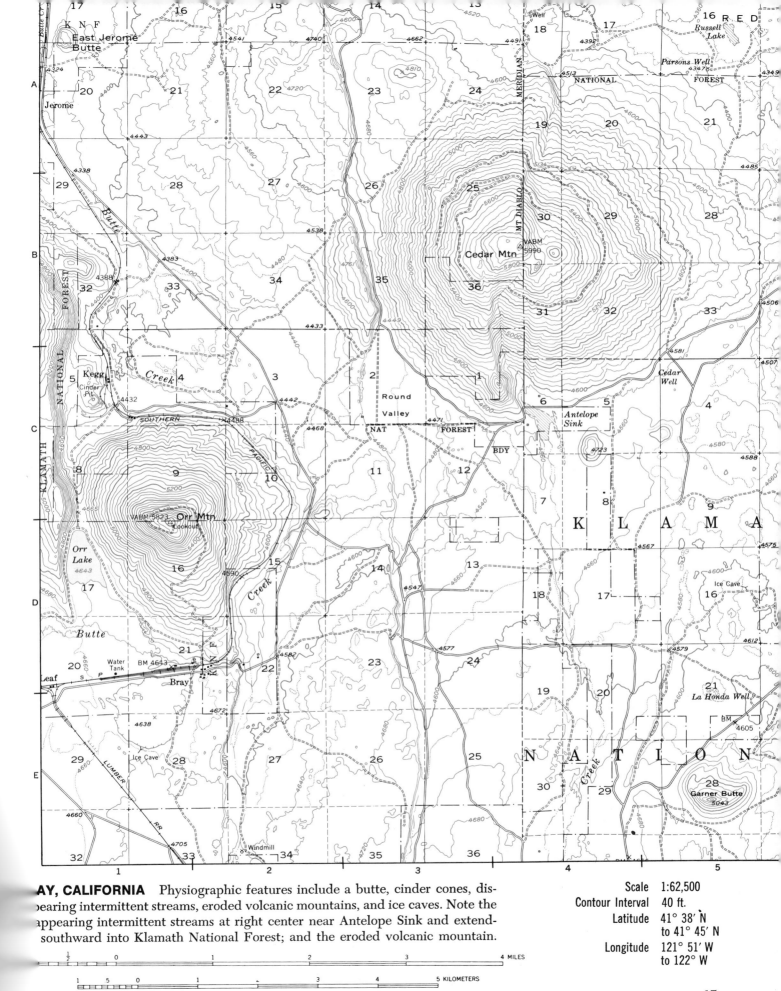

AY, CALIFORNIA Physiographic features include a butte, cinder cones, disappearing intermittent streams, eroded volcanic mountains, and ice caves. Note the appearing intermittent streams at right center near Antelope Sink and extend-southward into Klamath National Forest; and the eroded volcanic mountain.

Scale 1:62,500
Contour Interval 40 ft.
Latitude 41° 38′ N
 to 41° 45′ N
Longitude 121° 51′ W
 to 122° W

4 MILES

5 KILOMETERS

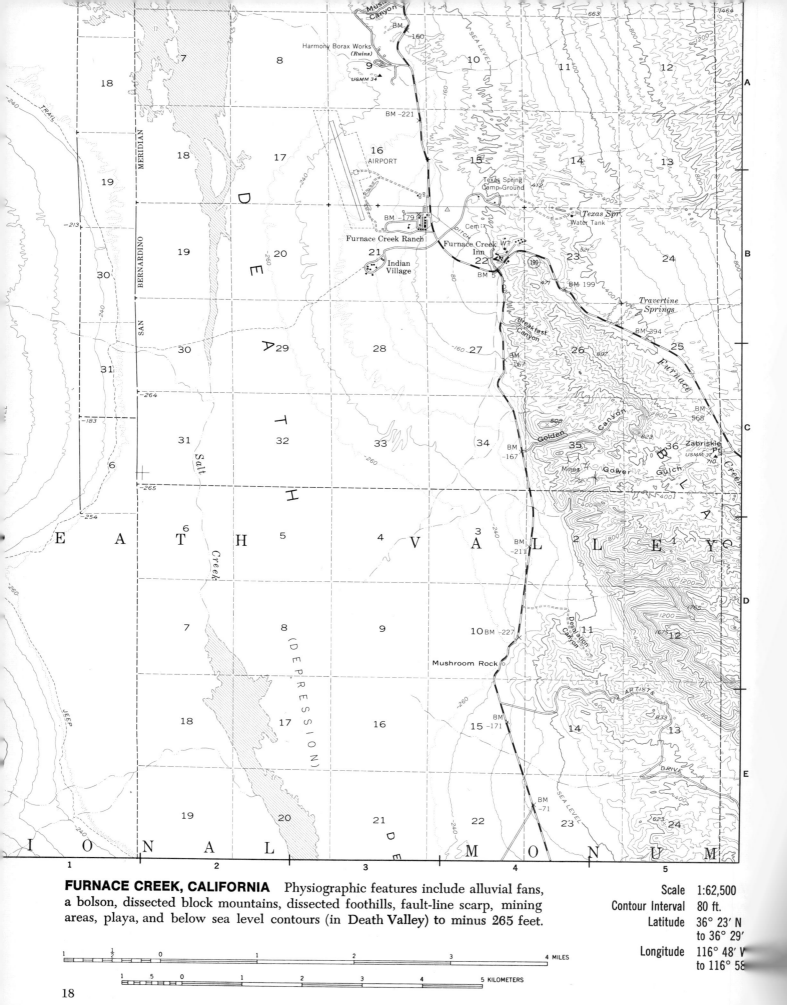

FURNACE CREEK, CALIFORNIA Physiographic features include alluvial fans, a bolson, dissected block mountains, dissected foothills, fault-line scarp, mining areas, playa, and below sea level contours (in Death Valley) to minus 265 feet.

Scale	1:62,500
Contour Interval	80 ft.
Latitude	36° 23′ N to 36° 29′
Longitude	116° 48′ W to 116° 58′

1   ½   0   1   2   3   4 MILES

1   5   0   1   2   3   4   5 KILOMETERS

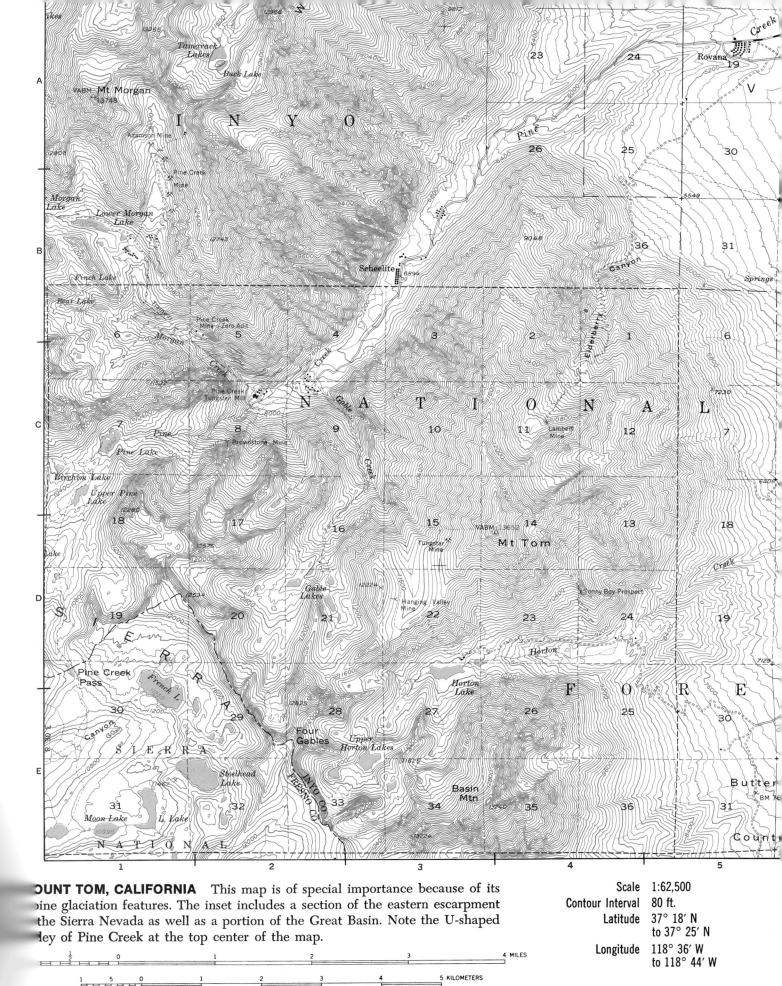

OUNT TOM, CALIFORNIA This map is of special importance because of its pine glaciation features. The inset includes a section of the eastern escarpment the Sierra Nevada as well as a portion of the Great Basin. Note the U-shaped ley of Pine Creek at the top center of the map.

Scale 1:62,500
Contour Interval 80 ft.
Latitude 37° 18′ N
to 37° 25′ N
Longitude 118° 36′ W
to 118° 44′ W

4 MILES

5 KILOMETERS

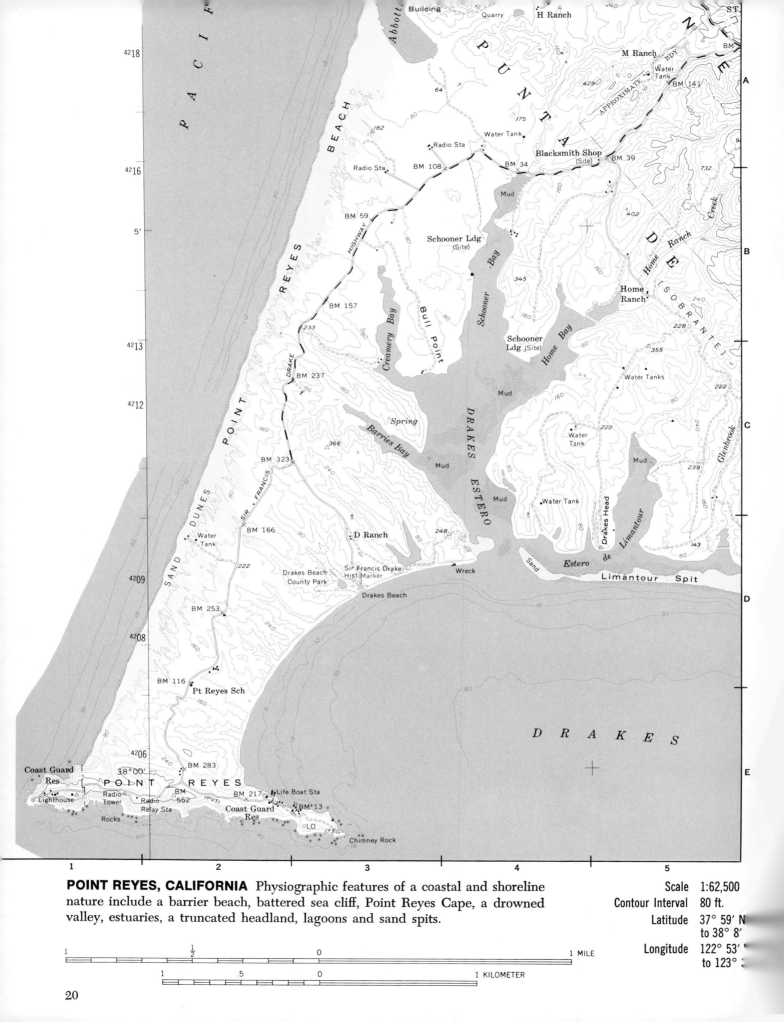

POINT REYES, CALIFORNIA Physiographic features of a coastal and shoreline nature include a barrier beach, battered sea cliff, Point Reyes Cape, a drowned valley, estuaries, a truncated headland, lagoons and sand spits.

Scale	1:62,500
Contour Interval	80 ft.
Latitude	37° 59′ N to 38° 8′
Longitude	122° 53′ to 123°

1   ½   0   1 MILE

1   .5   0   1 KILOMETER

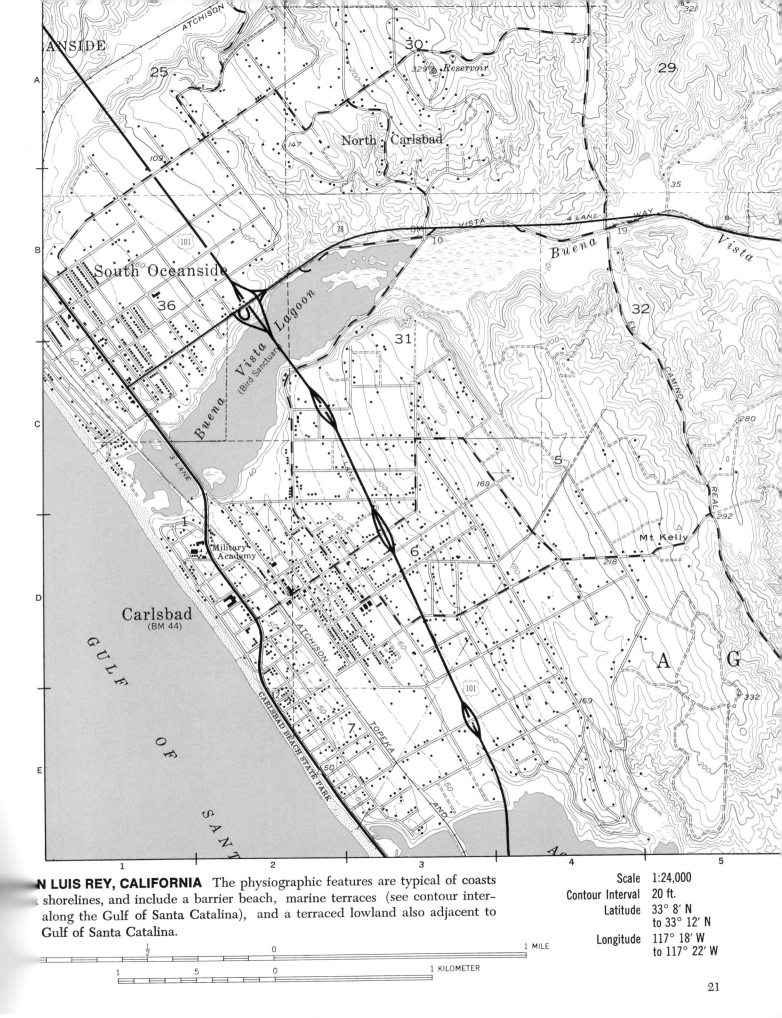

N LUIS REY, CALIFORNIA The physiographic features are typical of coasts
shorelines, and include a barrier beach, marine terraces (see contour inter-
along the Gulf of Santa Catalina), and a terraced lowland also adjacent to
Gulf of Santa Catalina.

Scale 1:24,000
Contour Interval 20 ft.
Latitude 33° 8′ N
to 33° 12′ N
Longitude 117° 18′ W
to 117° 22′ W

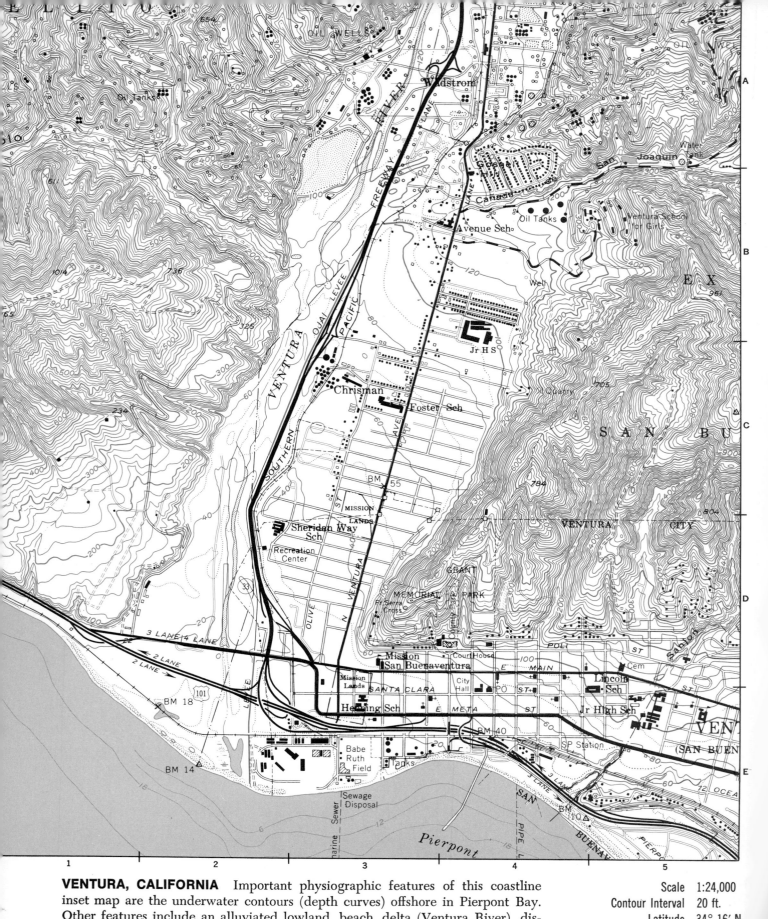

VENTURA, CALIFORNIA Important physiographic features of this coastline inset map are the underwater contours (depth curves) offshore in Pierpont Bay. Other features include an alluviated lowland, beach, delta (Ventura River), dissected upland, an oil field, and a river in a flood plain with a sand channel.

Scale 1:24,000
Contour Interval 20 ft.
Latitude 34° 16′ N
to 34° 19′
Longitude 119° 16′ W
to 119° 19′

1   ½   0   1 MILE
1   .5   0   1 KILOMETER

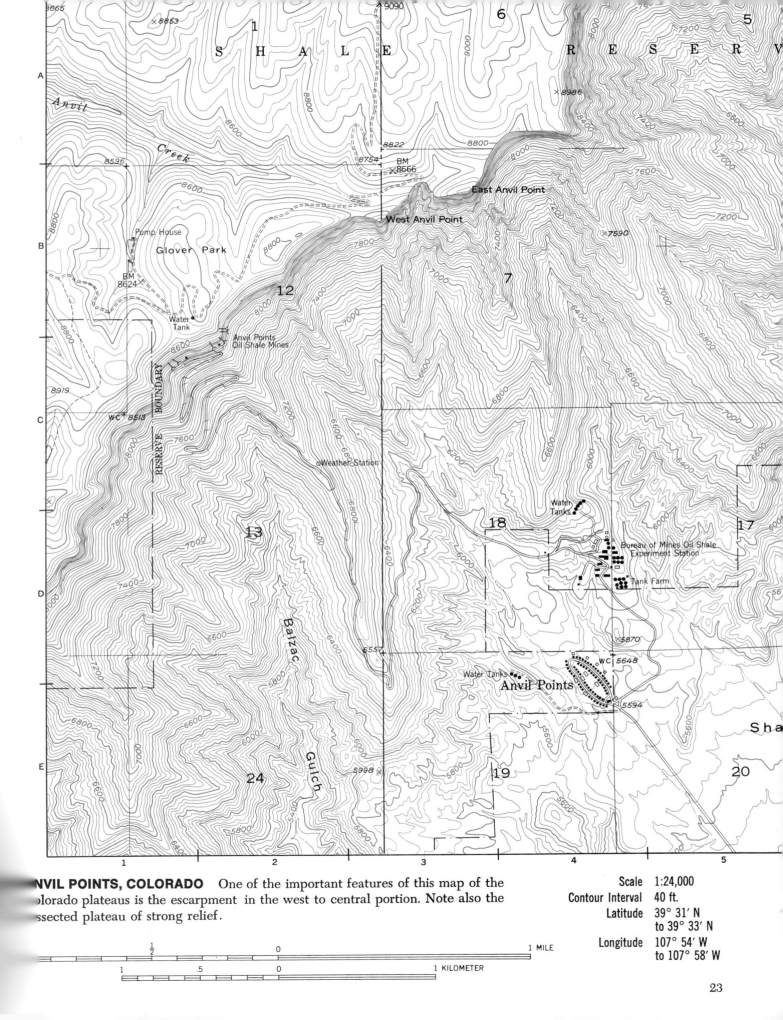

NVIL POINTS, COLORADO One of the important features of this map of the olorado plateaus is the escarpment in the west to central portion. Note also the ssected plateau of strong relief.

Scale 1:24,000
Contour Interval 40 ft.
Latitude 39° 31′ N
to 39° 33′ N
Longitude 107° 54′ W
to 107° 58′ W

MILE

1 KILOMETER

23

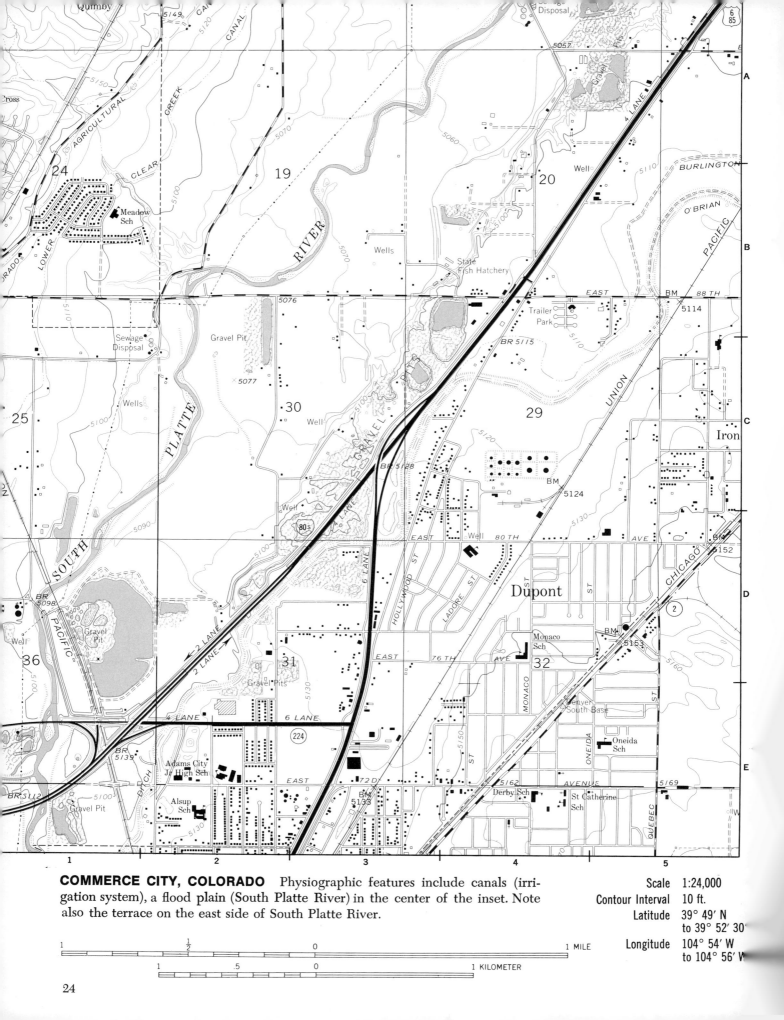

COMMERCE CITY, COLORADO Physiographic features include canals (irrigation system), a flood plain (South Platte River) in the center of the inset. Note also the terrace on the east side of South Platte River.

Scale 1:24,000
Contour Interval 10 ft.
Latitude 39° 49′ N
to 39° 52′ 30
Longitude 104° 54′ W
to 104° 56′ W

1   ½   0   1 MILE

1   .5   0   1 KILOMETER

24

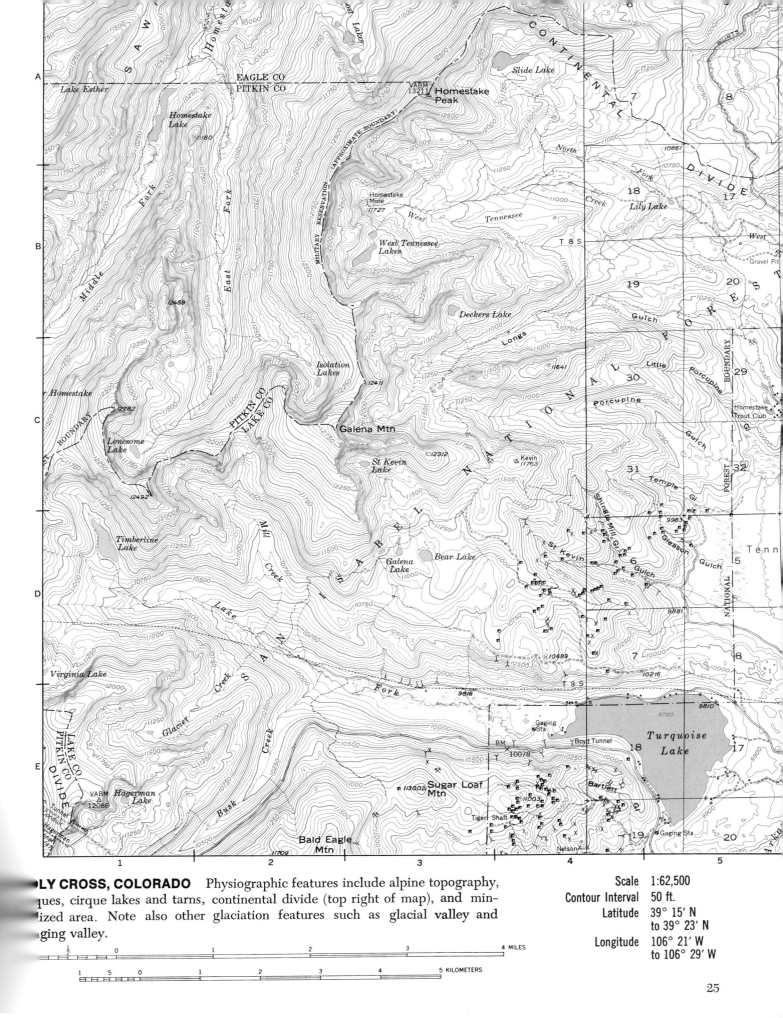

LY CROSS, COLORADO Physiographic features include alpine topography, ques, cirque lakes and tarns, continental divide (top right of map), and min-ized area. Note also other glaciation features such as glacial valley and ging valley.

Scale 1:62,500
Contour Interval 50 ft.
Latitude 39° 15′ N
to 39° 23′ N
Longitude 106° 21′ W
to 106° 29′ W

25

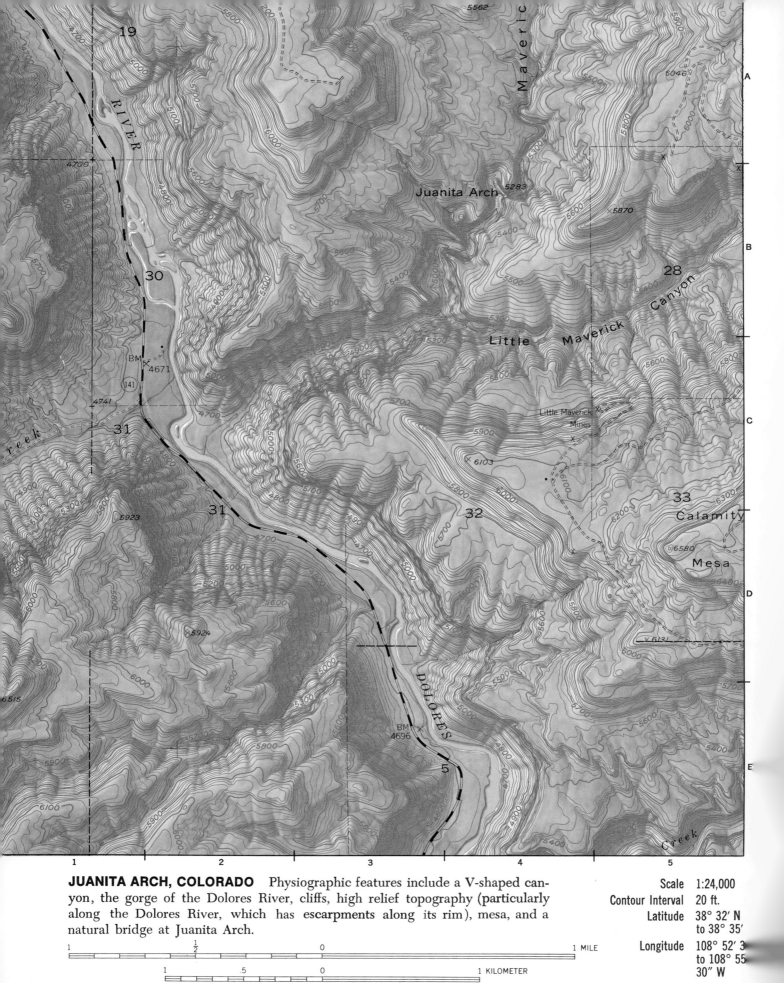

JUANITA ARCH, COLORADO Physiographic features include a V-shaped canyon, the gorge of the Dolores River, cliffs, high relief topography (particularly along the Dolores River, which has escarpments along its rim), mesa, and a natural bridge at Juanita Arch.

Scale 1:24,000
Contour Interval 20 ft.
Latitude 38° 32′ N
to 38° 35′
Longitude 108° 52′ 3
to 108° 55′
30″ W

1 MILE

1 KILOMETER

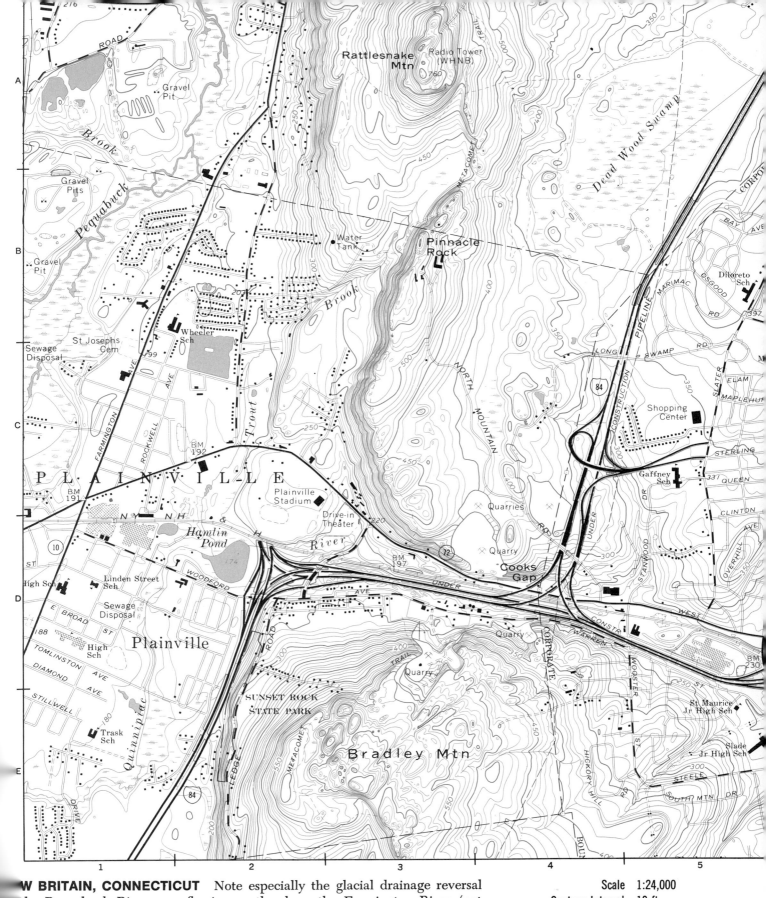

W BRITAIN, CONNECTICUT Note especially the glacial drainage reversal the Pequabuck River now flowing north where the Farmington River (not wn on the inset map) formerly flowed south. Other features include kettles, mlins, an ancient wind and water gap, stream piracy, and swamps.

Scale 1:24,000
Contour Interval 10 ft.
Latitude 41° 39′ N
to 41° 42′ N
Longitude 72° 49′ W
to 72° 52′ W

½   0   1 MILE

1   .5   0   1 KILOMETER

27

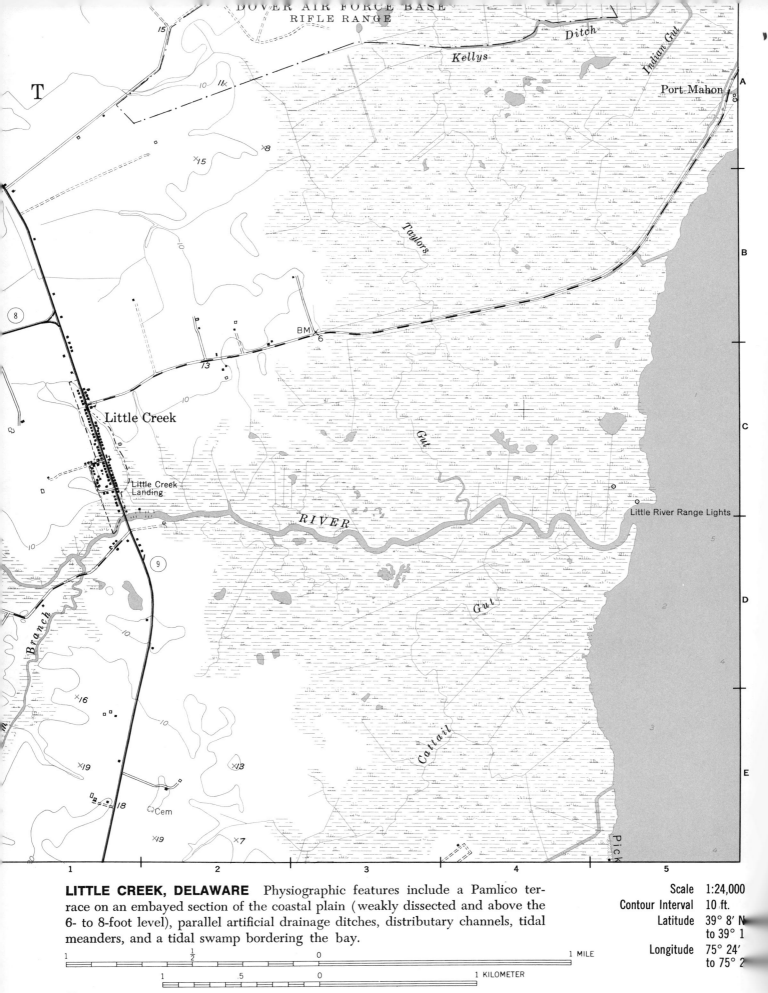

LITTLE CREEK, DELAWARE Physiographic features include a Pamlico terrace on an embayed section of the coastal plain (weakly dissected and above the 6- to 8-foot level), parallel artificial drainage ditches, distributary channels, tidal meanders, and a tidal swamp bordering the bay.

Scale 1:24,000
Contour Interval 10 ft.
Latitude 39° 8′ N
to 39° 1
Longitude 75° 24′
to 75° 2

1 MILE

1 KILOMETER

ASHINGTON WEST, D.C./VIRGINIA Physiographic features include a dis-
...ted depositional and erosional surface (Coastal Plain and Piedmont), a drowned
...er (Potomac below Key Bridge). Note also various cultural additions such as a
...nnel for small ships, and the urban area.

Scale	1:24,000
Contour Interval	10 ft.
Latitude	38° 53′ N
	to 38° 56′ N
Longitude	77° 2′ W
	to 77° 5′ W

1 MILE

1 KILOMETER

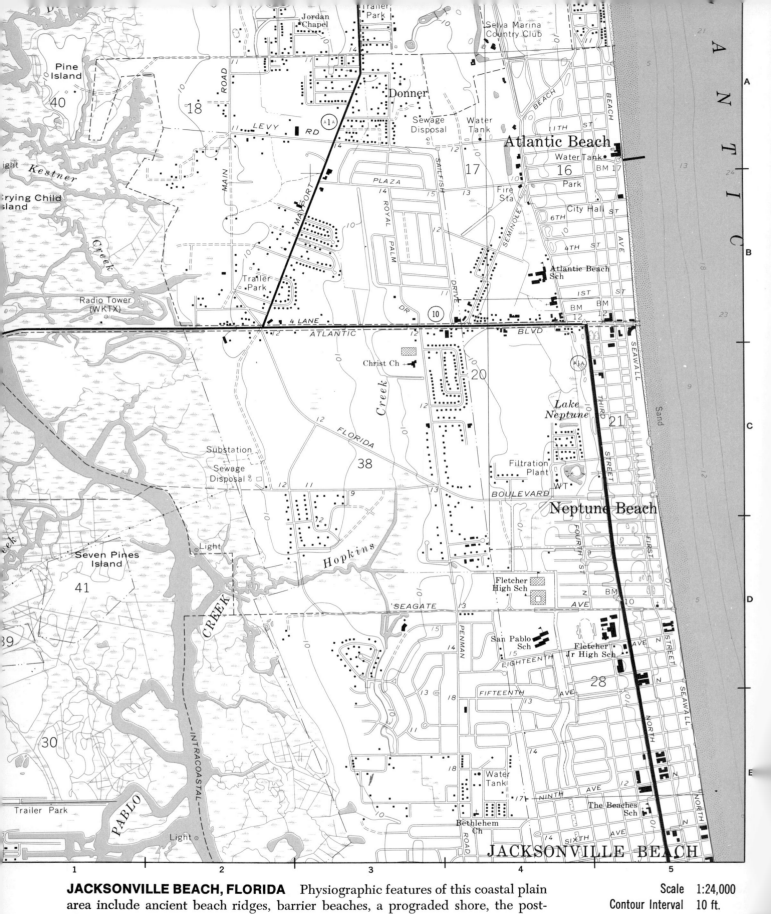

JACKSONVILLE BEACH, FLORIDA Physiographic features of this coastal plain area include ancient beach ridges, barrier beaches, a prograded shore, the post-Pleistocene shoreline (western portion of map at 6- to 8-foot level), and tidal swamp of Silver Bluff lagoon along the Intracoastal Waterway.

Scale	1:24,000	
Contour Interval	10 ft.	
Latitude	30° 17′ 30	
	to 30° 20′	
Longitude	81° 23′ W	
	to 81° 26′	

1   ½   0   1 MILE

1   .5   0   1 KILOMETER

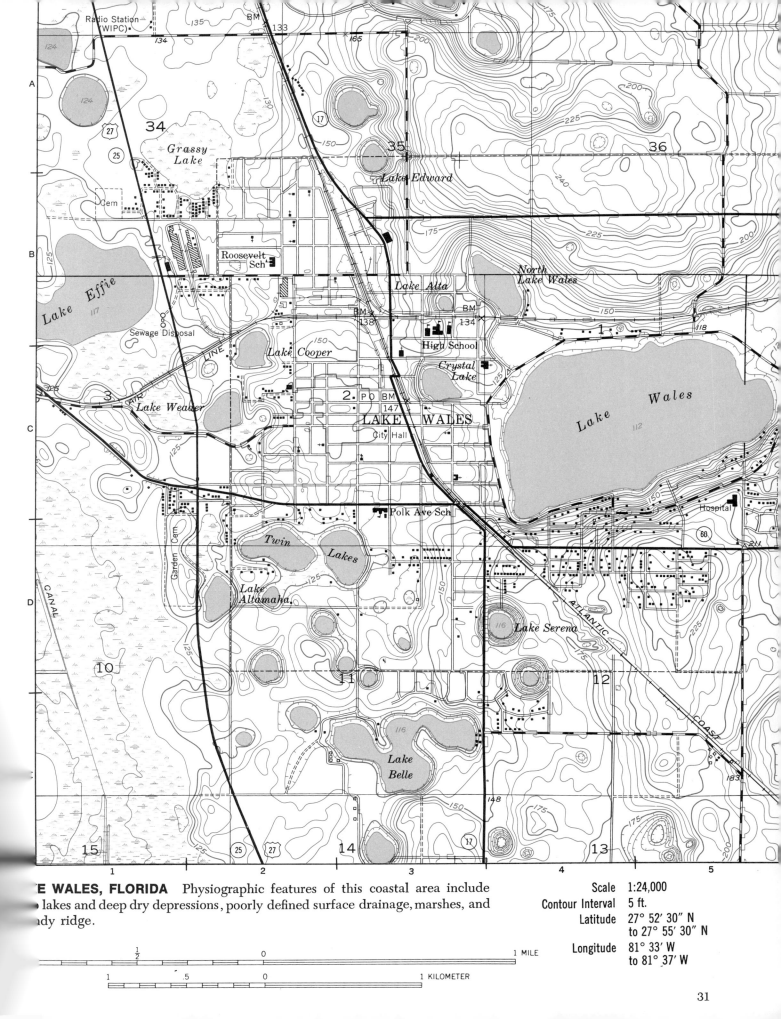

LAKE WALES, FLORIDA Physiographic features of this coastal area include lakes and deep dry depressions, poorly defined surface drainage, marshes, and sandy ridge.

Scale 1:24,000
Contour Interval 5 ft.
Latitude 27° 52′ 30″ N to 27° 55′ 30″ N
Longitude 81° 33′ W to 81° 37′ W

1 MILE

1 KILOMETER

WARM SPRINGS, GEORGIA Physiographic features include a basin eroded in soft rocks in a structural dome (The Cove at upper right, Pine Mountain), dissected peneplain surface, steeply dipping and folded resistant rock ridges (Pine Mountain region), superposed stream, water and wind gaps, and mineral springs.

Scale	1:62,50
Contour Interval	20 ft.
Latitude	32° 49'
	to 32°
Longitude	84° 30'
	to 84°

1   ½   0   1   2   3   4 MILES

1   5   0   1   2   3   4   5 KILOMETERS

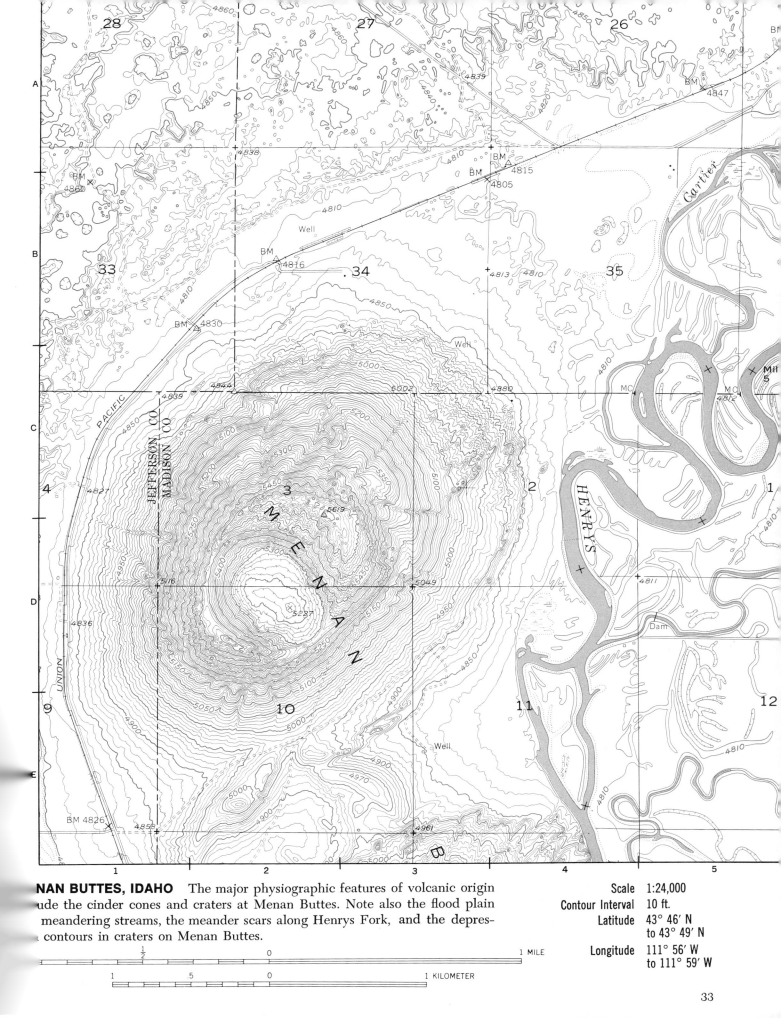

NAN BUTTES, IDAHO The major physiographic features of volcanic origin ...ude the cinder cones and craters at Menan Buttes. Note also the flood plain ... meandering streams, the meander scars along Henrys Fork, and the depres-... contours in craters on Menan Buttes.

Scale	1:24,000
Contour Interval	10 ft.
Latitude	43° 46′ N to 43° 49′ N
Longitude	111° 56′ W to 111° 59′ W

1 MILE

1 KILOMETER

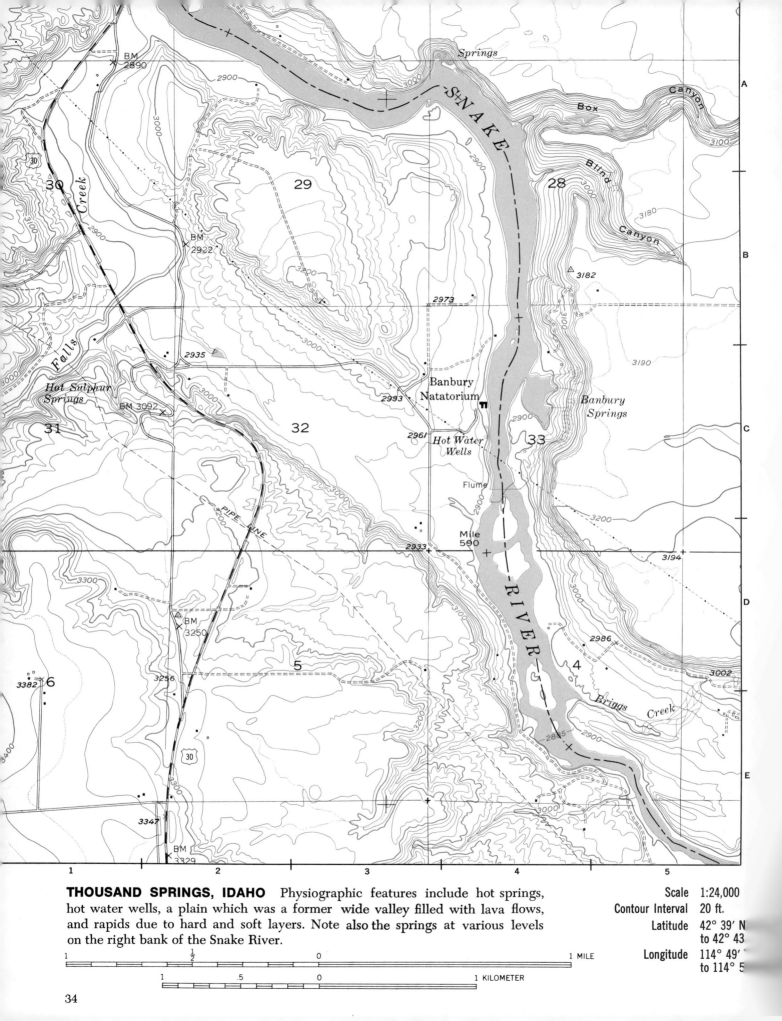

THOUSAND SPRINGS, IDAHO Physiographic features include hot springs, hot water wells, a plain which was a former wide valley filled with lava flows, and rapids due to hard and soft layers. Note also the springs at various levels on the right bank of the Snake River.

Scale 1:24,000
Contour Interval 20 ft.
Latitude 42° 39′ N to 42° 43
Longitude 114° 49′ to 114° 5

1 MILE

1 KILOMETER

34

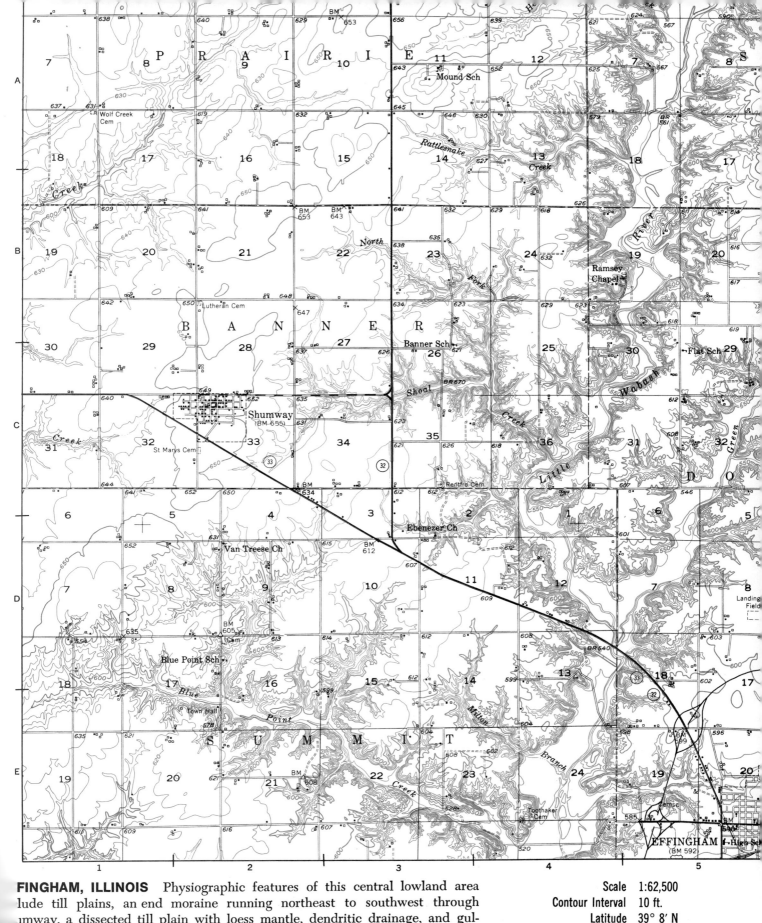

FINGHAM, ILLINOIS Physiographic features of this central lowland area
lude till plains, an end moraine running northeast to southwest through
imway, a dissected till plain with loess mantle, dendritic drainage, and gul-
d stream channels in flood plains.

Scale 1:62,500

Contour Interval 10 ft.

Latitude 39° 8' N
to 39° 15' N

Longitude 88° 33' W
to 88° 42' W

35

OOLITIC, INDIANA Physiographic features include interior low plateaus, abandoned meander (at Crooked Creek in the southwest portion of the map), dissected plateau, entrenched meanders (White River), meander core and spurs, slipoff and undercut slope, and a disappearing stream.

Scale 1:62,500
Contour Interval 20 ft.
Latitude 38° 47′
to 38° 5
Longitude 86° 31′
to 86°

4 MILES

5 KILOMETERS

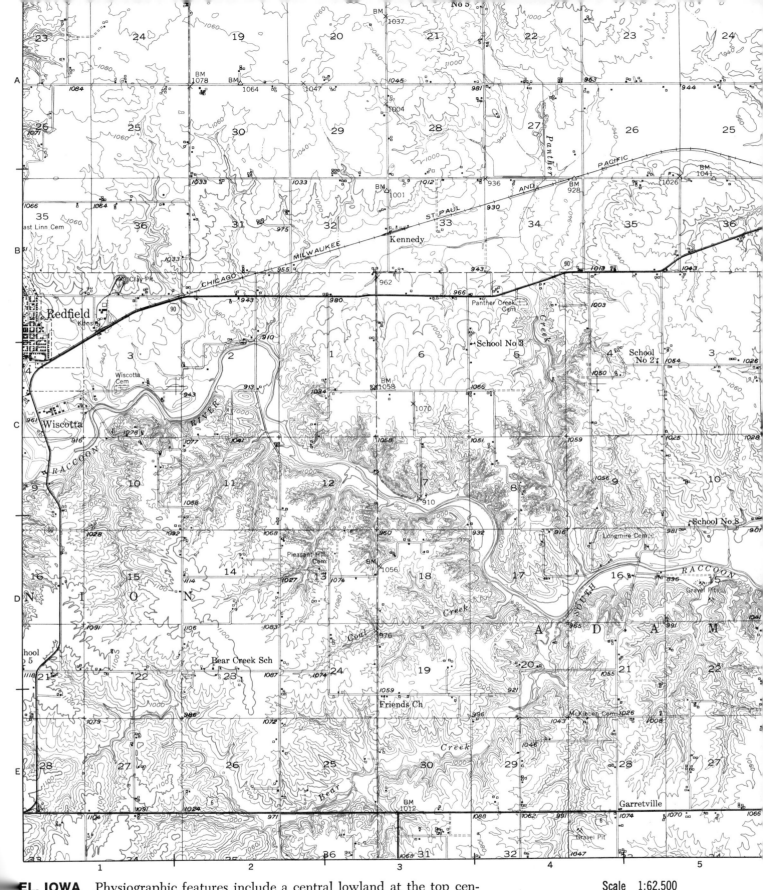

EL, IOWA Physiographic features include a central lowland at the top center of the map, dissected till plain, cutoff meander, dendritic drainage, former r channel (note contour intervals along and around C.M.St.P.&P. RR.), and am capture (Panther Creek, right center of the map, north to south).

Scale	1:62,500
Contour Interval	20 ft.
Latitude	41° 31′ N to 41° 38′ N
Longitude	94° 3′ W to 94° 12′ W

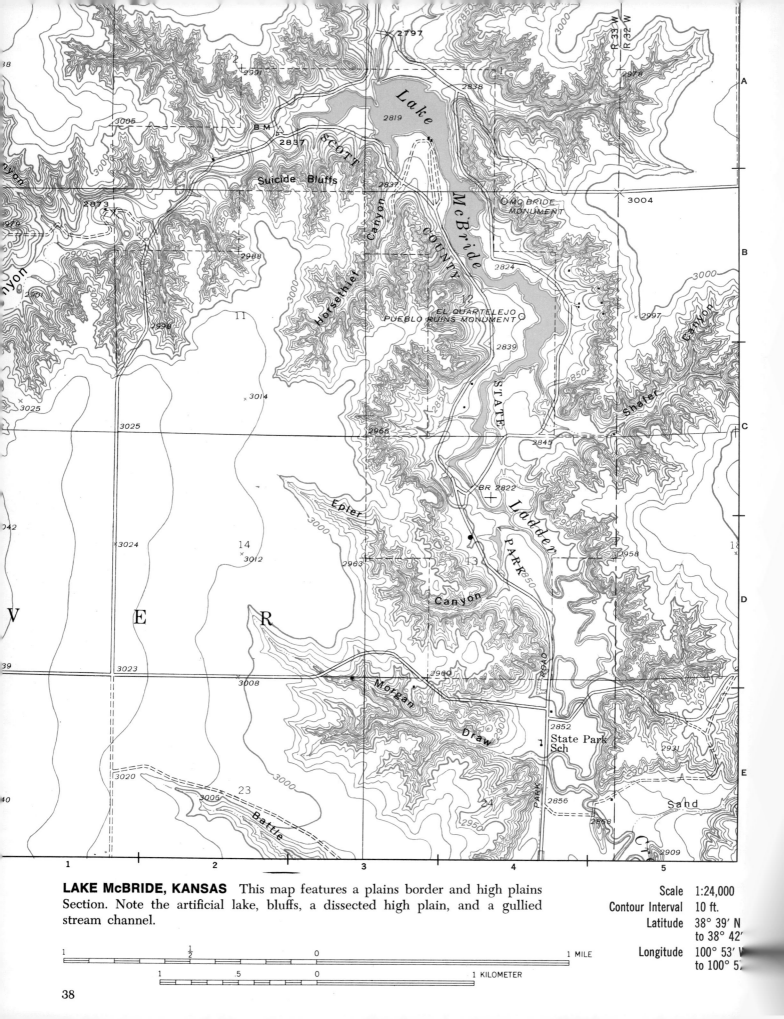

LAKE McBRIDE, KANSAS This map features a plains border and high plains Section. Note the artificial lake, bluffs, a dissected high plain, and a gullied stream channel.

Scale 1:24,000
Contour Interval 10 ft.
Latitude 38° 39' N to 38° 42'
Longitude 100° 53' W to 100° 5

1 MILE

1 KILOMETER

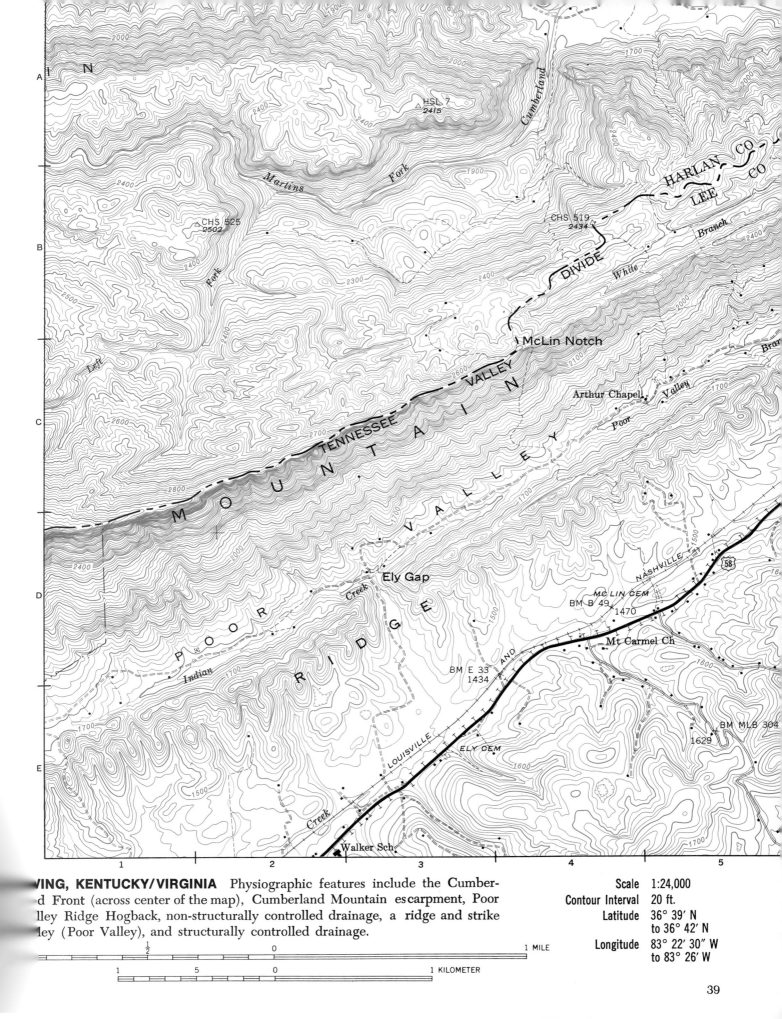

VING, KENTUCKY/VIRGINIA Physiographic features include the Cumber- d Front (across center of the map), Cumberland Mountain escarpment, Poor lley Ridge Hogback, non-structurally controlled drainage, a ridge and strike ley (Poor Valley), and structurally controlled drainage.

Scale	1:24,000
Contour Interval	20 ft.
Latitude	36° 39′ N to 36° 42′ N
Longitude	83° 22′ 30″ W to 83° 26′ W

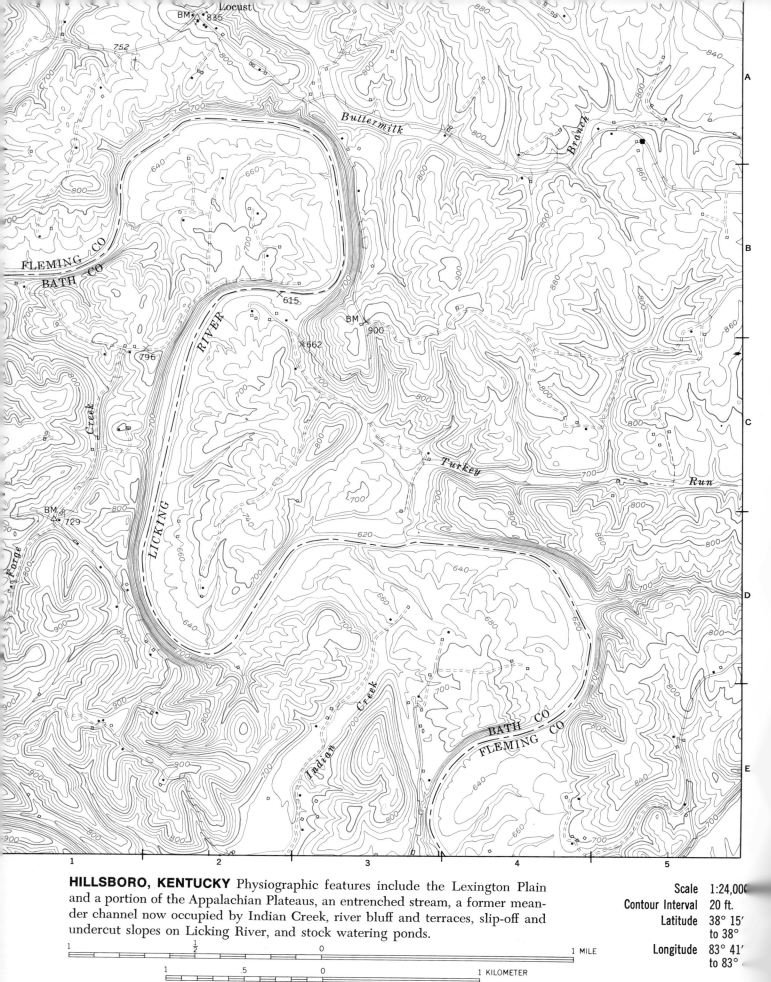

HILLSBORO, KENTUCKY Physiographic features include the Lexington Plain and a portion of the Appalachian Plateaus, an entrenched stream, a former meander channel now occupied by Indian Creek, river bluff and terraces, slip-off and undercut slopes on Licking River, and stock watering ponds.

Scale 1:24,000
Contour Interval 20 ft.
Latitude 38° 15′ to 38°
Longitude 83° 41′ to 83°

1 MILE

1 KILOMETER

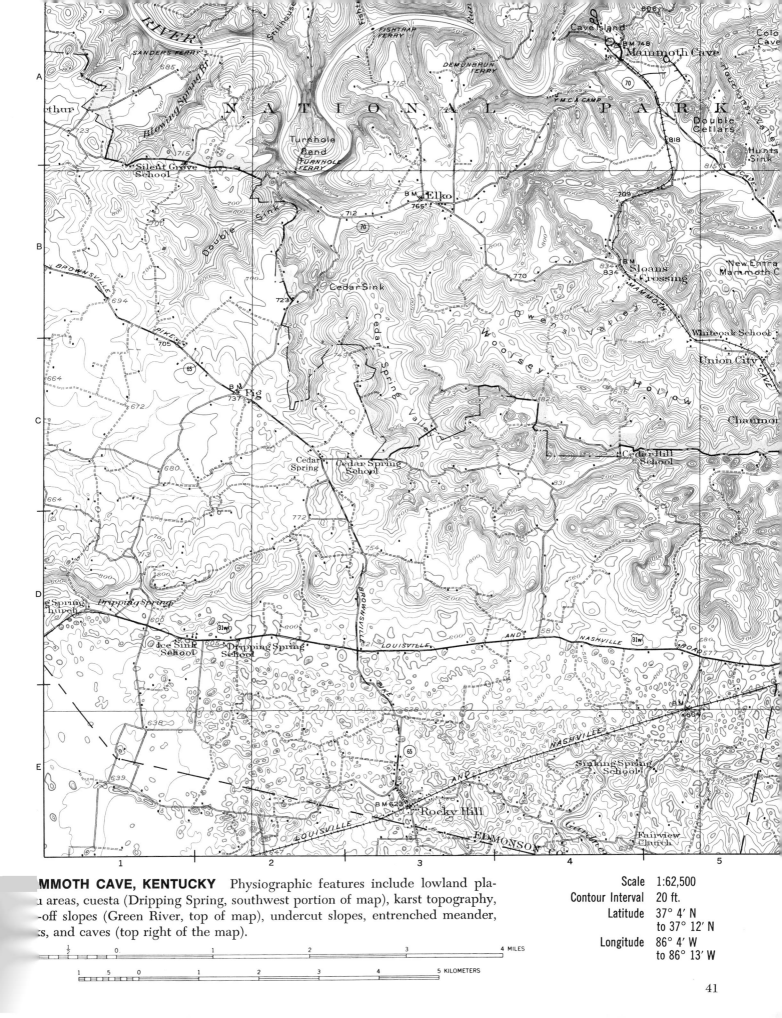

MMOTH CAVE, KENTUCKY Physiographic features include lowland pla-
areas, cuesta (Dripping Spring, southwest portion of map), karst topography,
-off slopes (Green River, top of map), undercut slopes, entrenched meander,
s, and caves (top right of the map).

Scale	1:62,500
Contour Interval	20 ft.
Latitude	37° 4' N
	to 37° 12' N
Longitude	86° 4' W
	to 86° 13' W

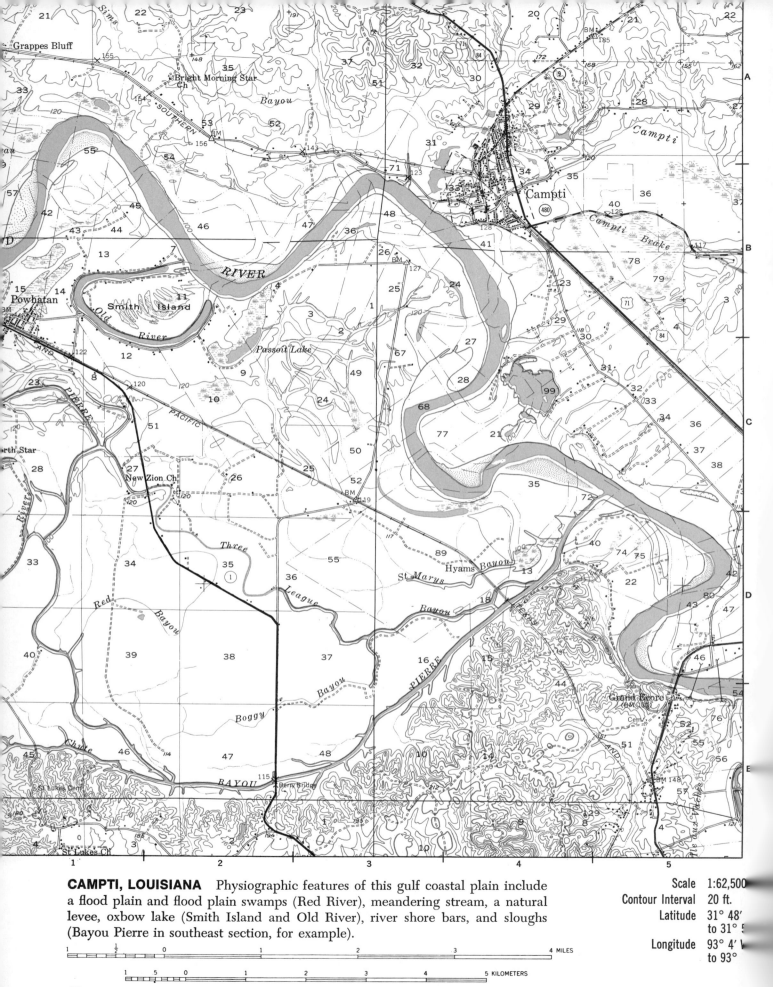

CAMPTI, LOUISIANA Physiographic features of this gulf coastal plain include a flood plain and flood plain swamps (Red River), meandering stream, a natural levee, oxbow lake (Smith Island and Old River), river shore bars, and sloughs (Bayou Pierre in southeast section, for example).

Scale 1:62,500
Contour Interval 20 ft.
Latitude 31° 48′
to 31° 5′
Longitude 93° 4′ W
to 93°

1   ½   0   1   2   3   4 MILES

1 5   0   1   2   3   4   5 KILOMETERS

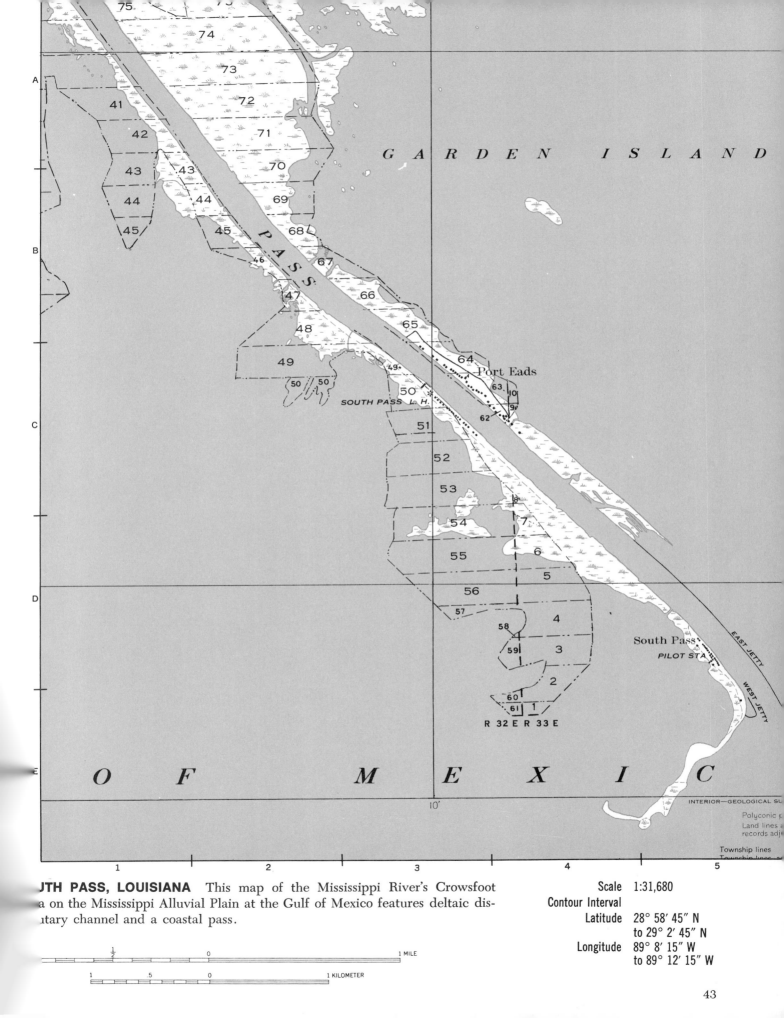

GARDEN ISLAND

Port Eads

SOUTH PASS L. H.

South Pass
PILOT STA.

EAST JETTY

WEST JETTY

R 32 E R 33 E

O F M E X I C

10'

INTERIOR—GEOLOGICAL SU

Polyconic p
Land lines a
records adj

Township lines
Township lines a

UTH PASS, LOUISIANA This map of the Mississippi River's Crowsfoot
a on the Mississippi Alluvial Plain at the Gulf of Mexico features deltaic dis-
tary channel and a coastal pass.

Scale 1:31,680
Contour Interval
Latitude 28° 58′ 45″ N
to 29° 2′ 45″ N
Longitude 89° 8′ 15″ W
to 89° 12′ 15″ W

1 MILE

1 KILOMETER

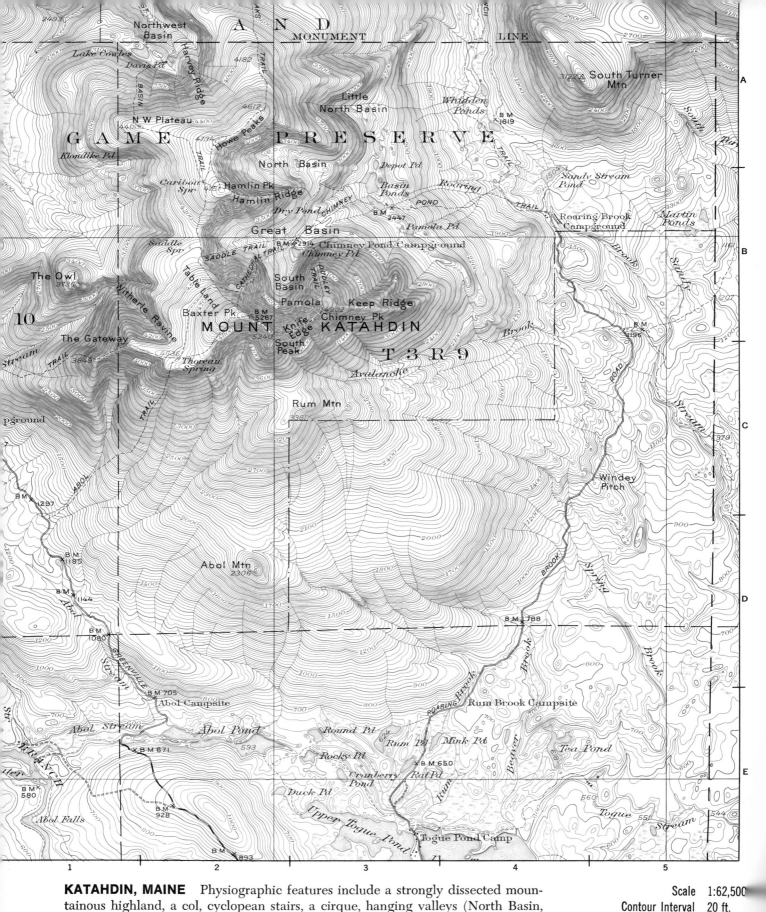

KATAHDIN, MAINE Physiographic features include a strongly dissected mountainous highland, a col, cyclopean stairs, a cirque, hanging valleys (North Basin, etc.), kames, a marsh, monadnock (Mount Katahdin), radial drainage, ponds in kettles, and waterfalls and rapids.

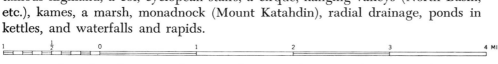

Scale 1:62,500

Contour Interval 20 ft.

Latitude 45° 49′
to 45° 5

Longitude 68° 49′
to 68°

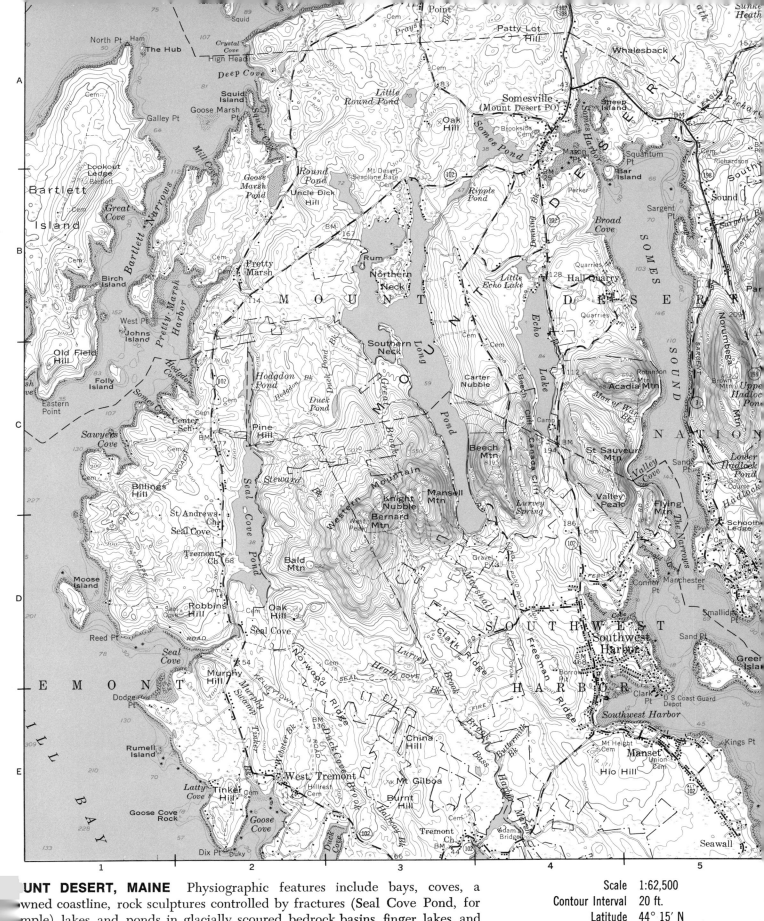

UNT DESERT, MAINE Physiographic features include bays, coves, a ~~w~~ned coastline, rock sculptures controlled by fractures (Seal Cove Pond, for ~~m~~ple), lakes and ponds in glacially scoured bedrock basins, finger lakes, and ~~r~~rows.

Scale	1:62,500
Contour Interval	20 ft.
Latitude	44° 15′ N
	to 44° 23′ N
Longitude	68° 17′ W
	to 68° 26′ W

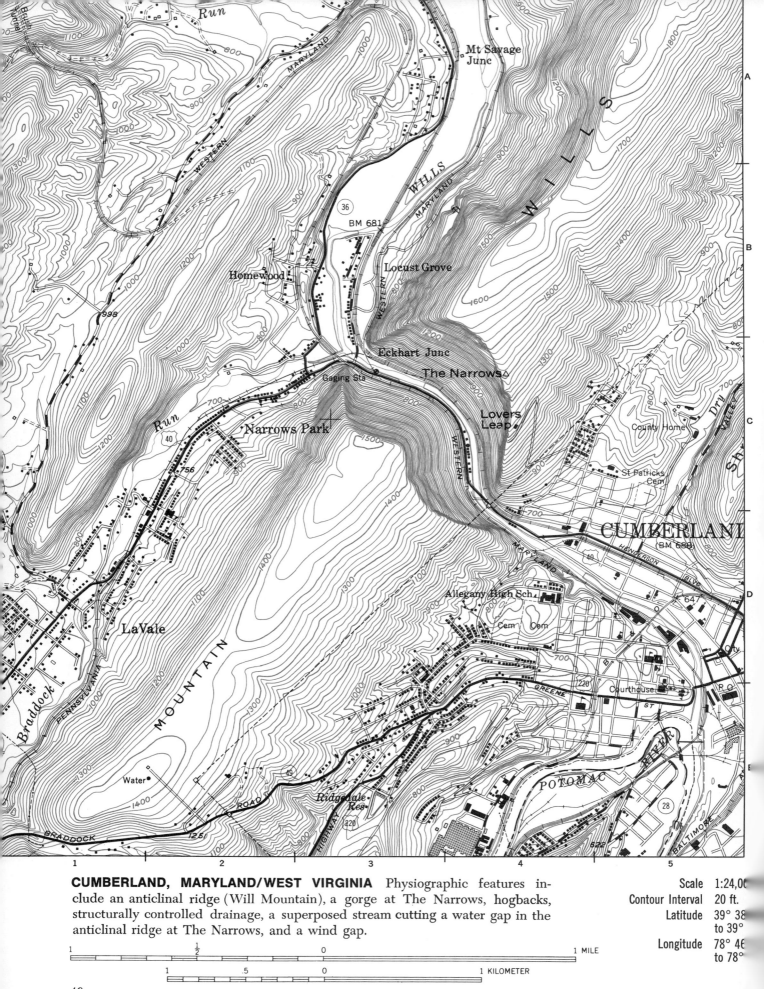

CUMBERLAND, MARYLAND/WEST VIRGINIA Physiographic features include an anticlinal ridge (Will Mountain), a gorge at The Narrows, hogbacks, structurally controlled drainage, a superposed stream cutting a water gap in the anticlinal ridge at The Narrows, and a wind gap.

Scale 1:24,0
Contour Interval 20 ft.
Latitude 39° 38
to 39°
Longitude 78° 46
to 78°

1   1/2   0   1 MILE

1   .5   0   1 KILOMETER

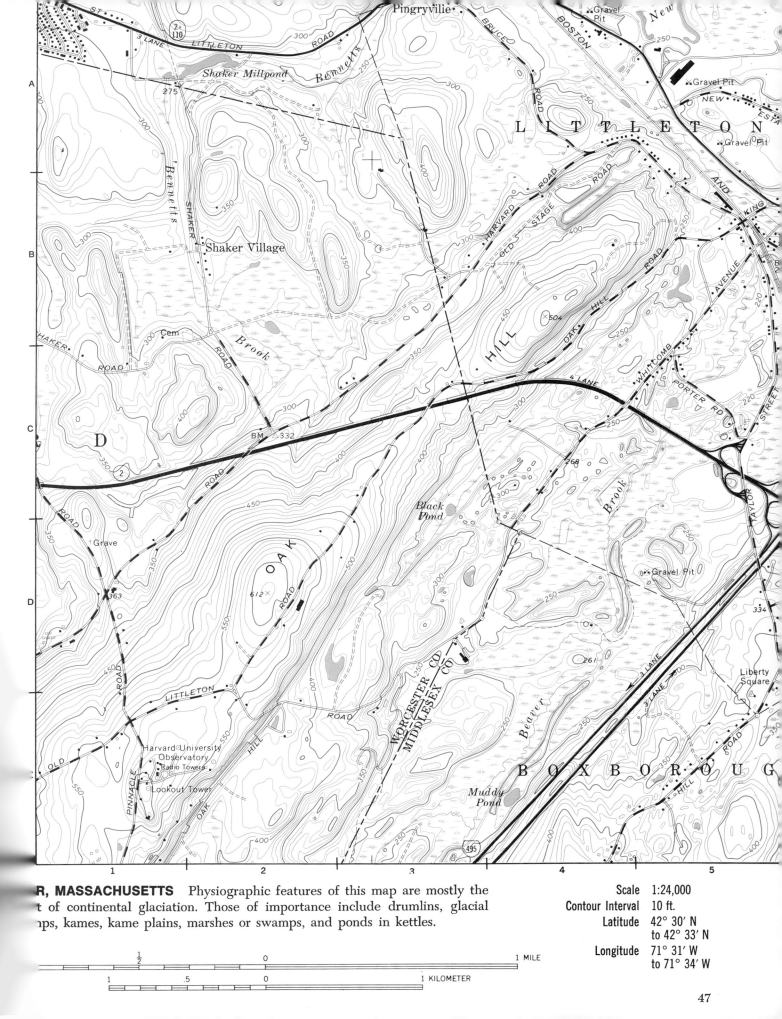

R, MASSACHUSETTS Physiographic features of this map are mostly the
[resul]t of continental glaciation. Those of importance include drumlins, glacial
[ka]mps, kames, kame plains, marshes or swamps, and ponds in kettles.

Scale 1:24,000
Contour Interval 10 ft.
Latitude 42° 30′ N
to 42° 33′ N
Longitude 71° 31′ W
to 71° 34′ W

½   0   1 MILE

1   .5   0   1 KILOMETER

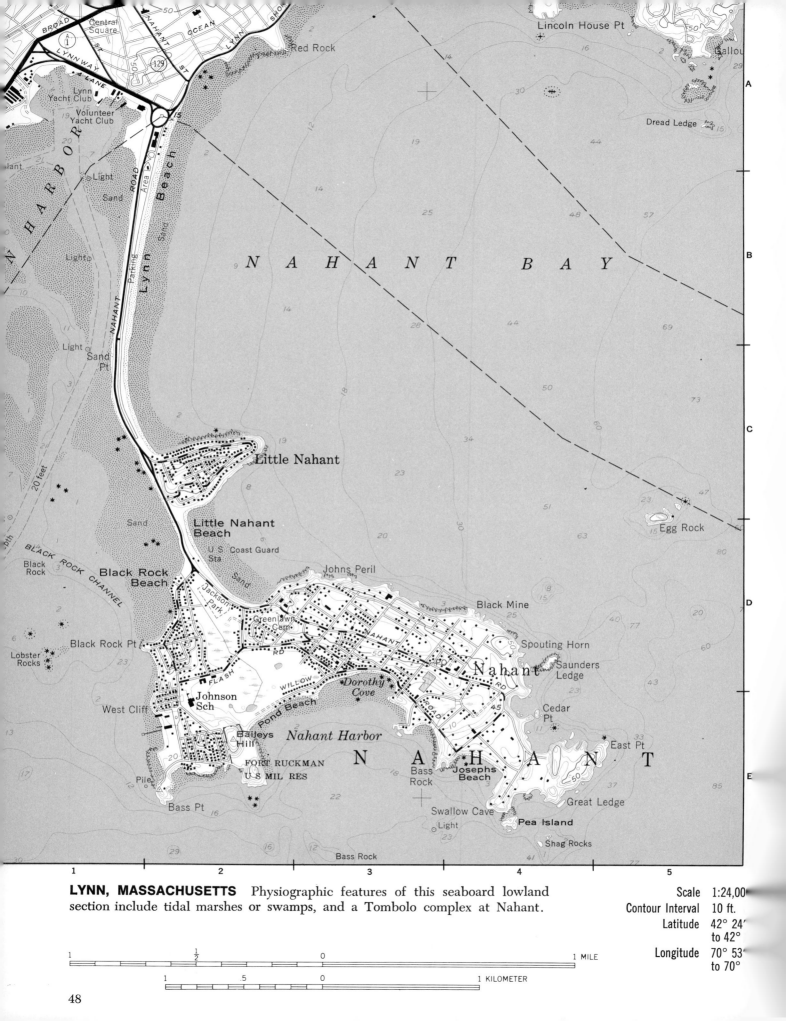

LYNN SHORE

Lincoln House Pt

Gallou

BROAD

Central
Square

NAHANT
OCEAN

129

LYNNWAY

Red Rock

Dread Ledge

A

Lynn
Yacht Club

Volunteer
Yacht Club

15

Light

Sand

N A H A N T   B A Y

B

HARBOR

Light

Parking
Area

Light

Sand
Pt

20 feet

BLACK ROCK CHANNEL

Light

Sand

C

Little Nahant

Little Nahant
Beach

Egg Rock

Black
Rock

Black Rock
Beach

U. S. Coast Guard
Sta

Sand

Johns Peril

Black Mine

D

Black Rock
Pt

Jackson
Park

Greenlawn
Cem.

NAHANT

Spouting Horn

Saunders
Ledge

Lobster
Rocks

FLASH

WILLOW

RD

Dorothy
Cove

Nahant

RD

Cedar
Pt

West Cliff

Johnson
Sch

Pond Beach

Nahant Harbor

ROAD

East Pt

Baileys
Hill

N A H A N T

Josephs
Beach

Great Ledge

E

Pile

FORT RUCKMAN
U S MIL RES

Bass
Rock

Swallow Cave

Pea Island

Bass Pt

Light

Shag Rocks

Bass Rock

1   2   3   4   5

LYNN, MASSACHUSETTS Physiographic features of this seaboard lowland
section include tidal marshes or swamps, and a Tombolo complex at Nahant.

Scale   1:24,00
Contour Interval   10 ft.
Latitude   42° 24'
to 42°
Longitude   70° 53'
to 70°

1   ½   0   1 MILE

1   .5   0   1 KILOMETER

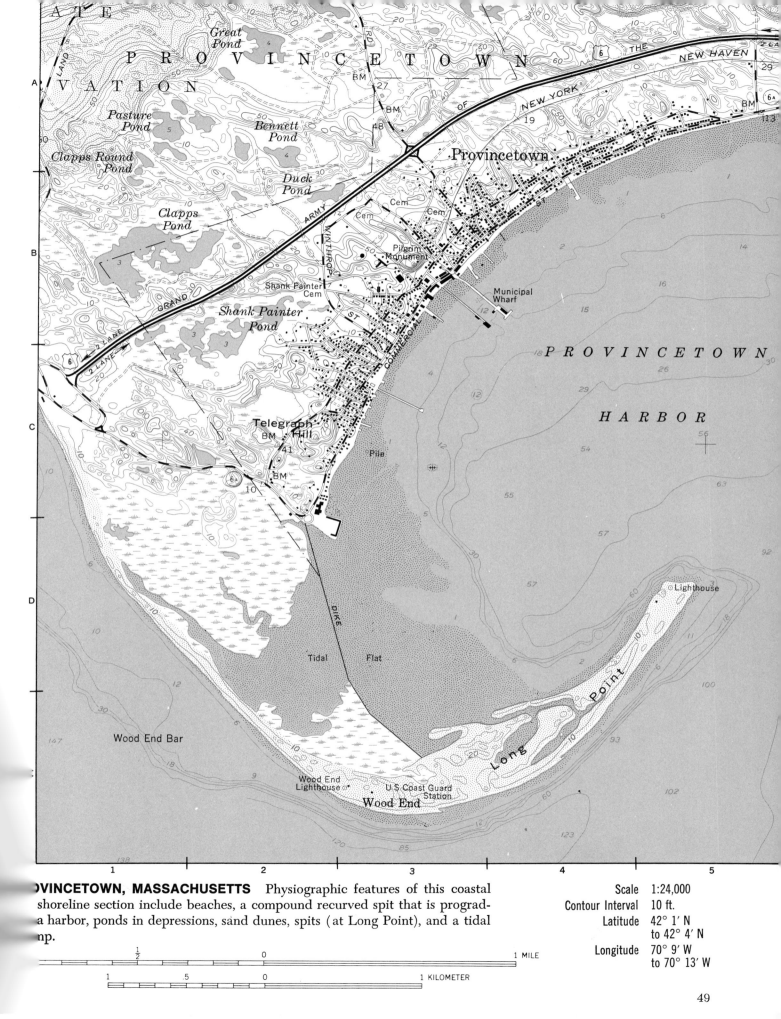

PROVINCETOWN, MASSACHUSETTS Physiographic features of this coastal shoreline section include beaches, a compound recurved spit that is prograding a harbor, ponds in depressions, sand dunes, spits (at Long Point), and a tidal ramp.

Scale 1:24,000

Contour Interval 10 ft.

Latitude 42° 1′ N to 42° 4′ N

Longitude 70° 9′ W to 70° 13′ W

½ 0 1 MILE

1 5 0 1 KILOMETER

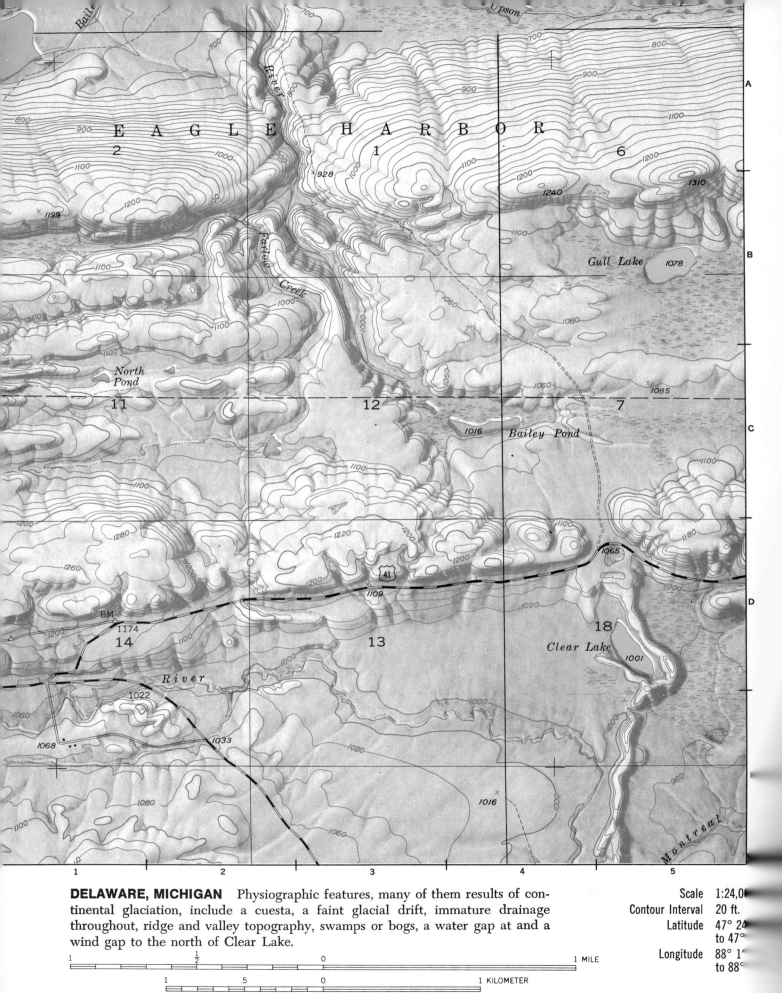

DELAWARE, MICHIGAN Physiographic features, many of them results of continental glaciation, include a cuesta, a faint glacial drift, immature drainage throughout, ridge and valley topography, swamps or bogs, a water gap at and a wind gap to the north of Clear Lake.

Scale 1:24,0
Contour Interval 20 ft.
Latitude 47° 24
to 47°
Longitude 88° 1
to 88°

1 MILE

1 KILOMETER

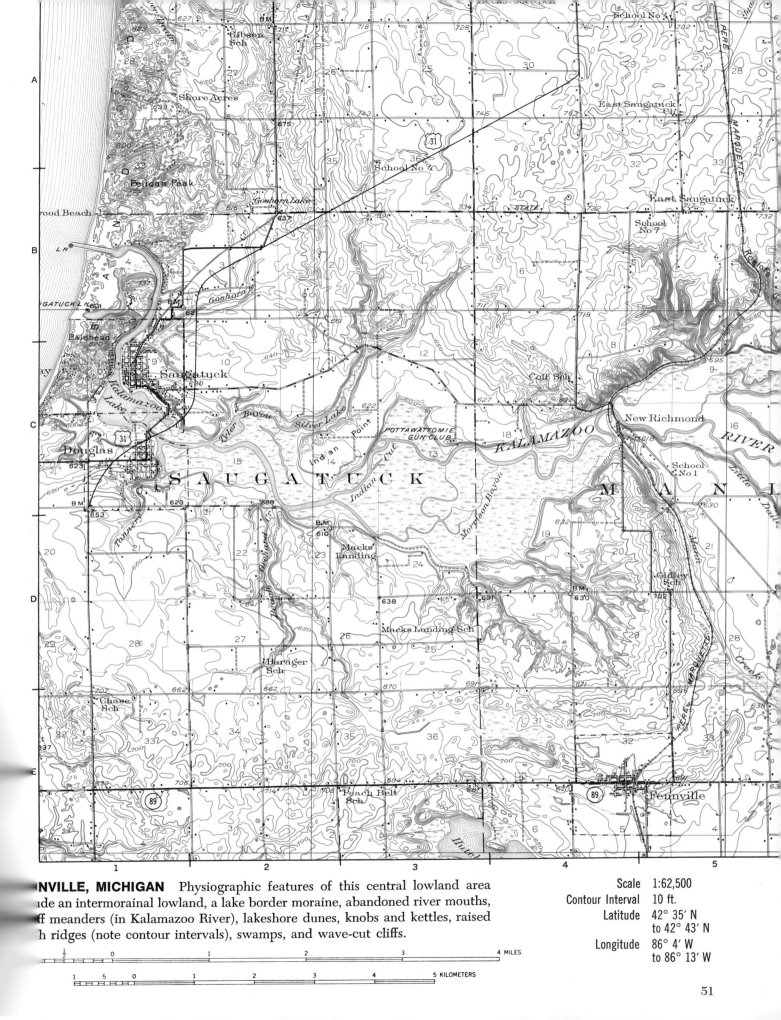

NVILLE, MICHIGAN Physiographic features of this central lowland area
de an intermorainal lowland, a lake border moraine, abandoned river mouths,
ff meanders (in Kalamazoo River), lakeshore dunes, knobs and kettles, raised
h ridges (note contour intervals), swamps, and wave-cut cliffs.

Scale	1:62,500
Contour Interval	10 ft.
Latitude	42° 35′ N
	to 42° 43′ N
Longitude	86° 4′ W
	to 86° 13′ W

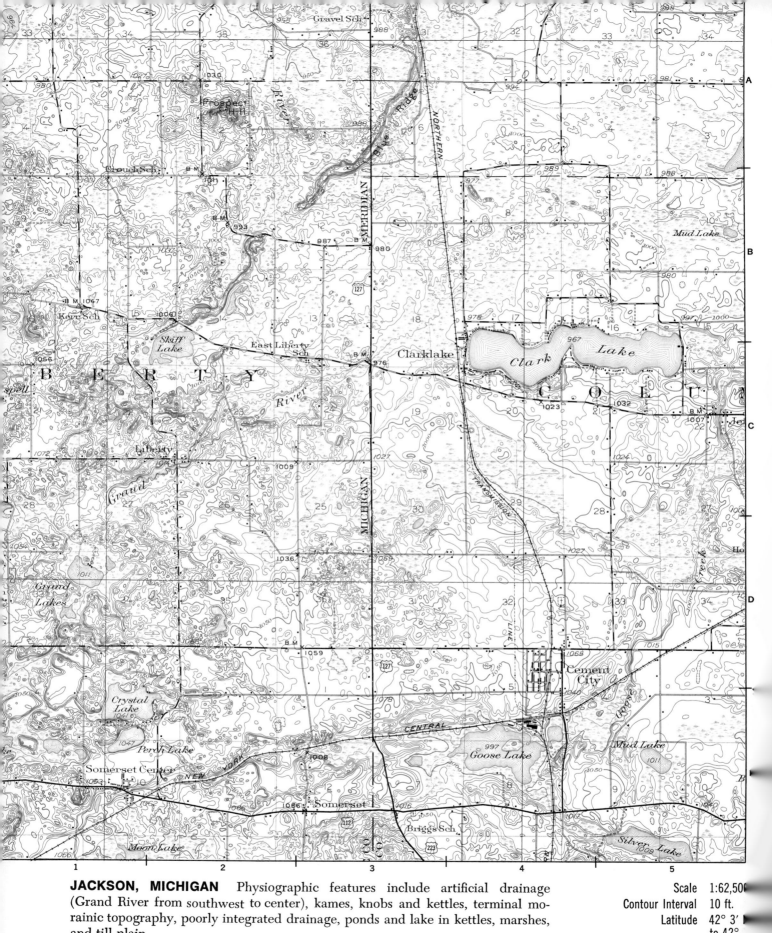

JACKSON, MICHIGAN Physiographic features include artificial drainage (Grand River from southwest to center), kames, knobs and kettles, terminal morainic topography, poorly integrated drainage, ponds and lake in kettles, marshes, and till plain.

Scale 1:62,50
Contour Interval 10 ft.
Latitude 42° 3'
to 42°
Longitude 84° 18
to 84°

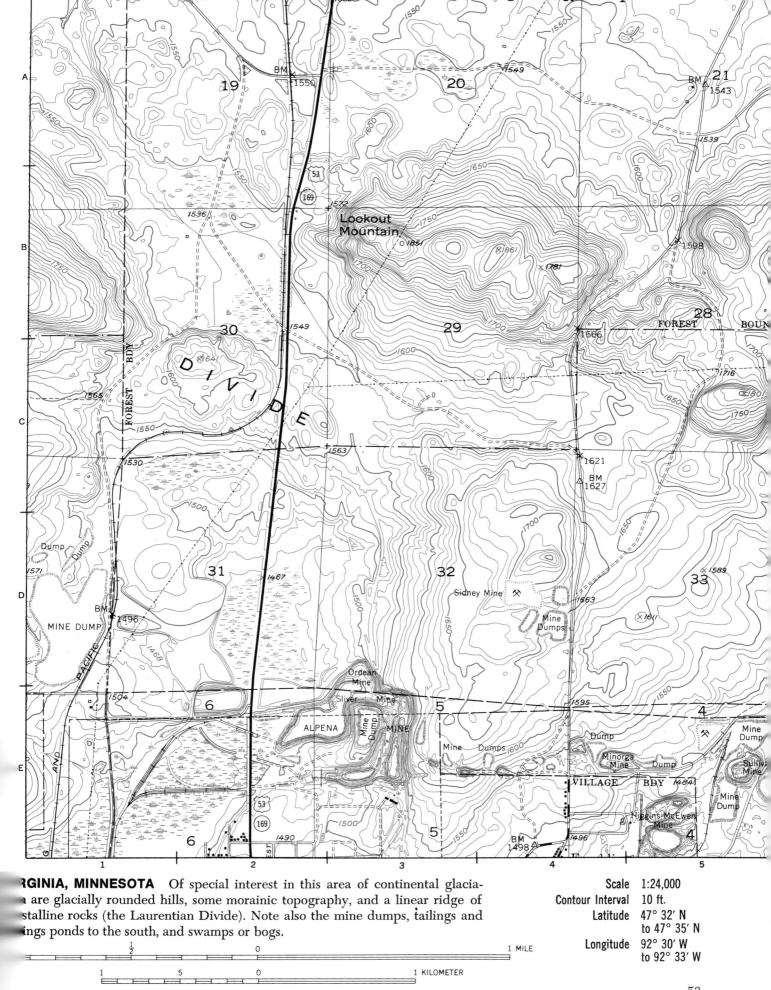

RGINIA, MINNESOTA Of special interest in this area of continental glacia-
 are glacially rounded hills, some morainic topography, and a linear ridge of
stalline rocks (the Laurentian Divide). Note also the mine dumps, tailings and
ings ponds to the south, and swamps or bogs.

Scale 1:24,000
Contour Interval 10 ft.
Latitude 47° 32′ N
to 47° 35′ N
Longitude 92° 30′ W
to 92° 33′ W

½ 0 1 MILE

1 .5 0 1 KILOMETER

53

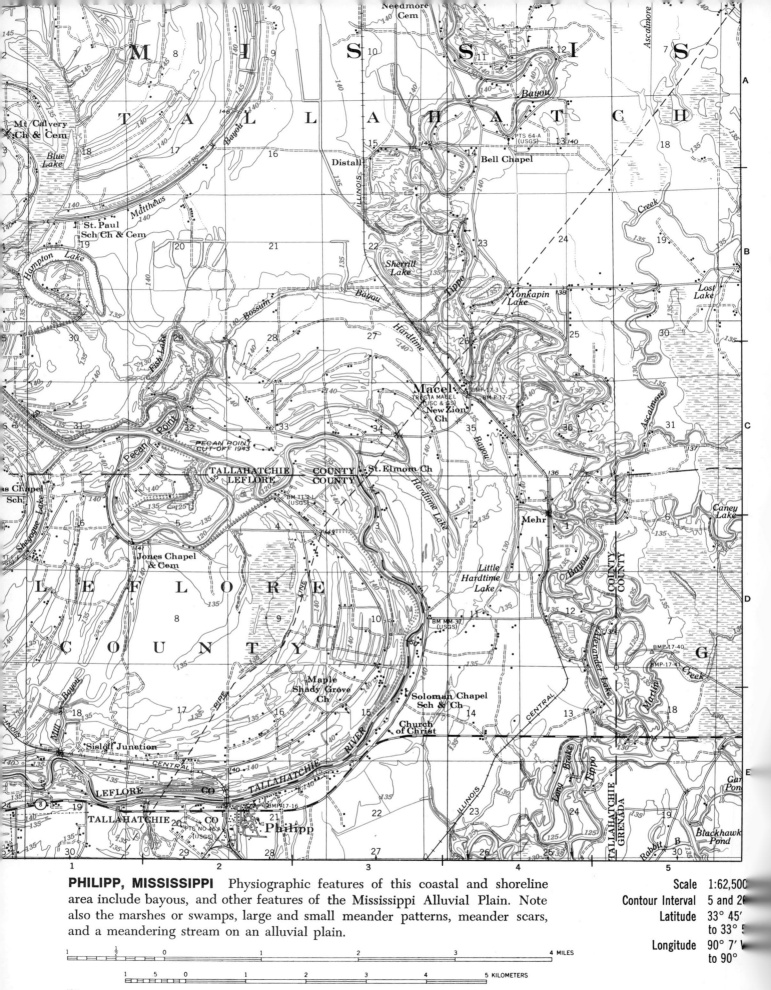

PHILIPP, MISSISSIPPI Physiographic features of this coastal and shoreline area include bayous, and other features of the Mississippi Alluvial Plain. Note also the marshes or swamps, large and small meander patterns, meander scars, and a meandering stream on an alluvial plain.

Scale 1:62,500

Contour Interval 5 and 20

Latitude 33° 45'
to 33° 5

Longitude 90° 7' W
to 90°

54

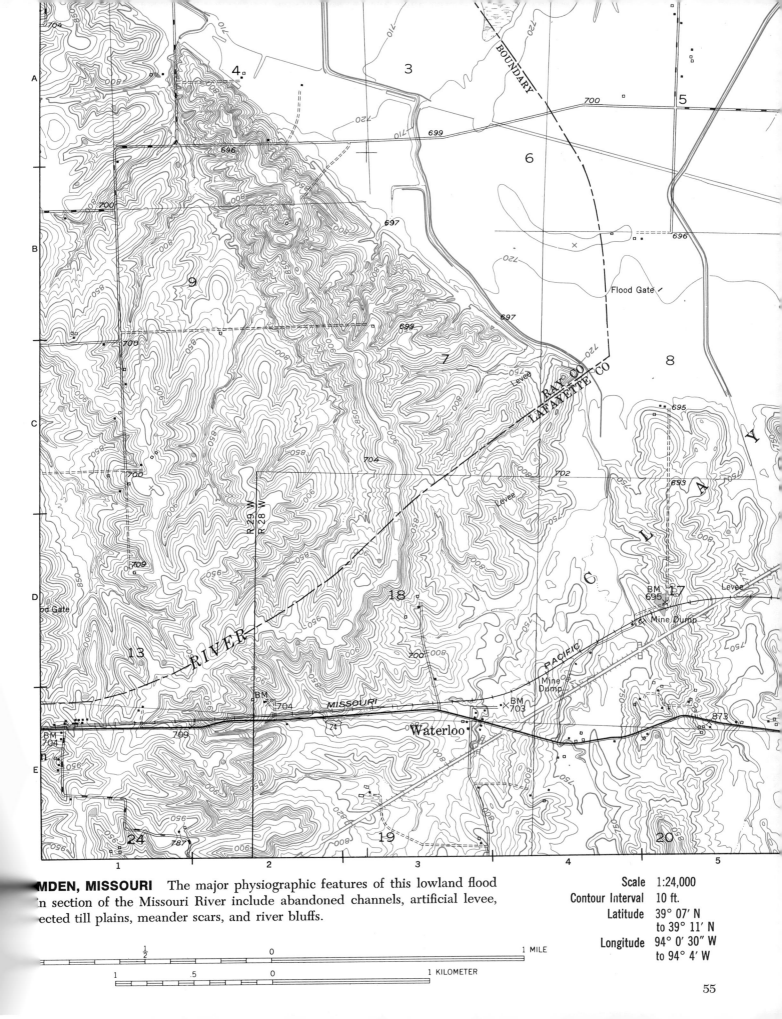

MDEN, MISSOURI The major physiographic features of this lowland flood
n section of the Missouri River include abandoned channels, artificial levee,
ected till plains, meander scars, and river bluffs.

Scale 1:24,000
Contour Interval 10 ft.
Latitude 39° 07′ N
to 39° 11′ N
Longitude 94° 0′ 30″ W
to 94° 4′ W

½   0   1 MILE

1   .5   0   1 KILOMETER

55

IRONTON, MISSOURI Physiographic features of this plateau region (known as the Iron Mountain Country) include the apex of the Ozark Plateau with dissected upland, non-glaciated knobs, and centripetal drainage (all of which originates within the USGS 15′ quadrangle map boundaries).

Scale 1:62,500

Contour Interval 20 ft.

Latitude 37° 35′ to 37°

Longitude 90° 32′ to 90°

56

CHIEF MOUNTAIN, MONTANA Physiographic features are primarily of alpine topography, including arêtes, cirques, cirque lakes, cols, cyclopean stairs, finger lakes, glaciers, and glacial troughs, hanging and U-shaped valleys, tarns, stream piracy, and a wind gap at Kootenai Pass.

Scale	1:125,000
Contour Interval	100 ft.
Latitude	48° 41′ N to 48° 57′ N
Longitude	113° 34′ W to 113° 54′ W

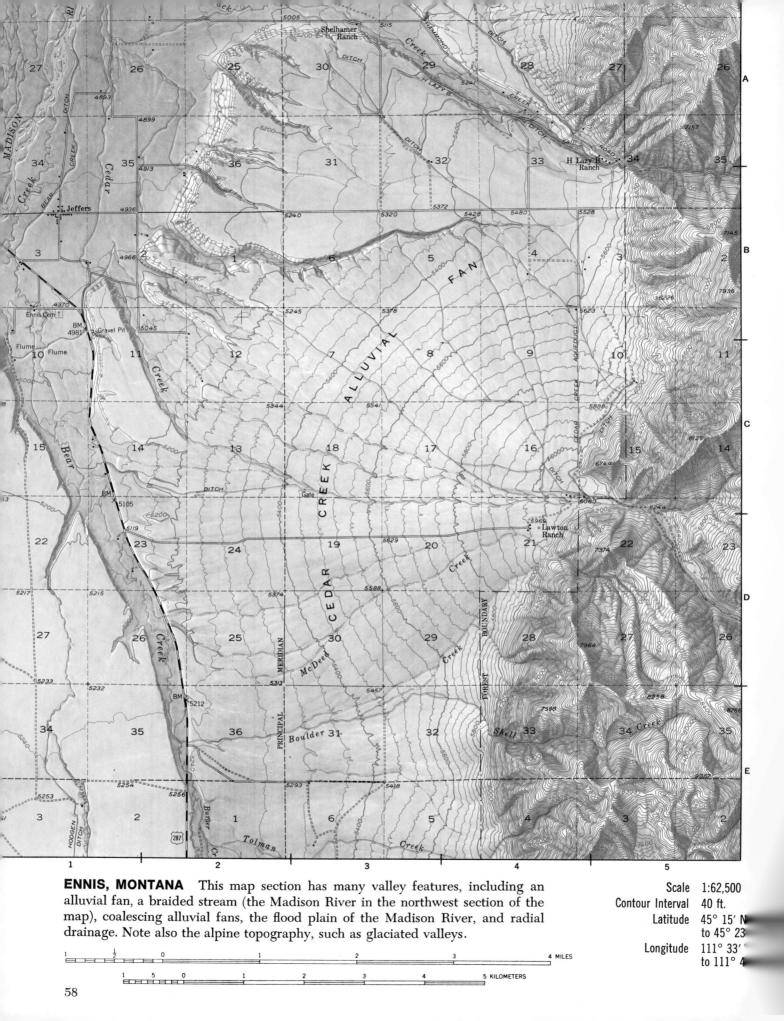

ENNIS, MONTANA This map section has many valley features, including an alluvial fan, a braided stream (the Madison River in the northwest section of the map), coalescing alluvial fans, the flood plain of the Madison River, and radial drainage. Note also the alpine topography, such as glaciated valleys.

Scale 1:62,500
Contour Interval 40 ft.
Latitude 45° 15′ N
to 45° 23′
Longitude 111° 33′
to 111° 4

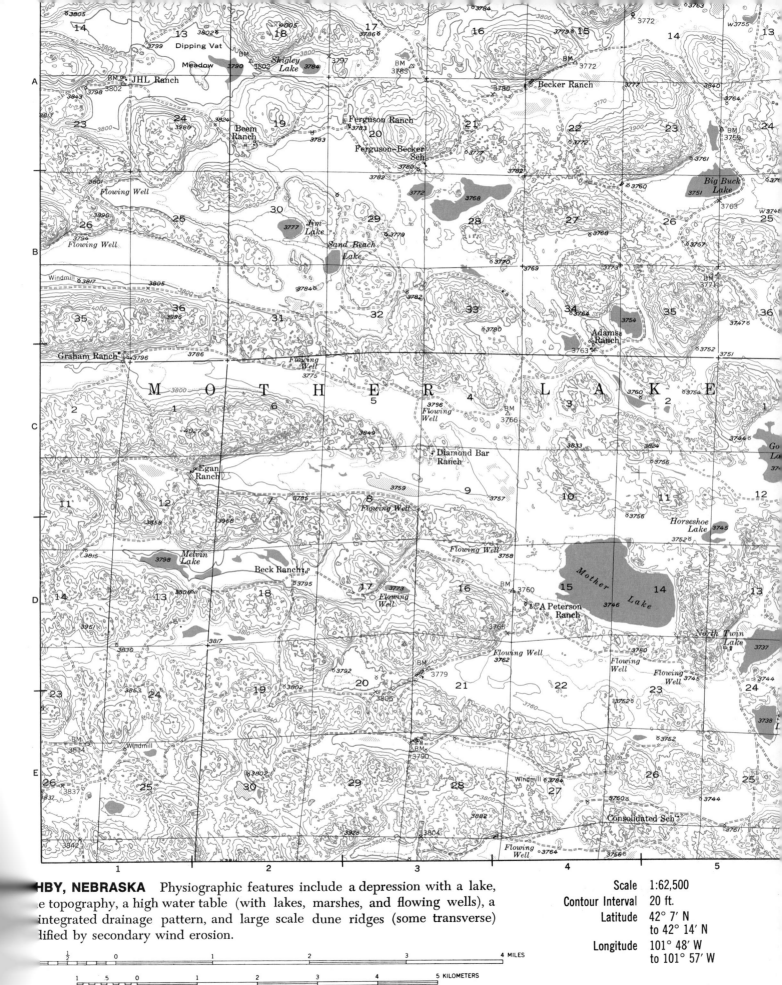

HBY, NEBRASKA Physiographic features include a depression with a lake,
e topography, a high water table (with lakes, marshes, and flowing wells), a
integrated drainage pattern, and large scale dune ridges (some transverse)
lified by secondary wind erosion.

Scale	1:62,500
Contour Interval	20 ft.
Latitude	42° 7′ N to 42° 14′ N
Longitude	101° 48′ W to 101° 57′ W

4 MILES

5 KILOMETERS

SONOMA RANGE, NEVADA Physiographic features of special significance on this map include dissected block mountains, bolsons, and playas. Note also the bajadas, flats, and numerous gaps and passes on the map.

Scale 1:250,000
Contour Interval 100 ft.
Latitude 40° 2′ N
to 40° 34′
Longitude 117° 5′ W
to 117° 40

AWFORD NOTCH, NEW HAMPSHIRE Physiographic features include bedk knobs, cascades, cirques, cliffs, dissected mountains of crystalline rocks overlen by glaciers, falls, a hanging valley, a notch, pond drainage, ridges, tarns, the U-shaped valley of the Saco River.

Scale	1:62,500
Contour Interval	20 ft.
Latitude	44° 5' N
	to 44° 13' N
Longitude	71° 18' W
	to 71° 28' W

½ 0 1 2 3 4 MILES

1 5 0 1 2 3 4 5 KILOMETERS

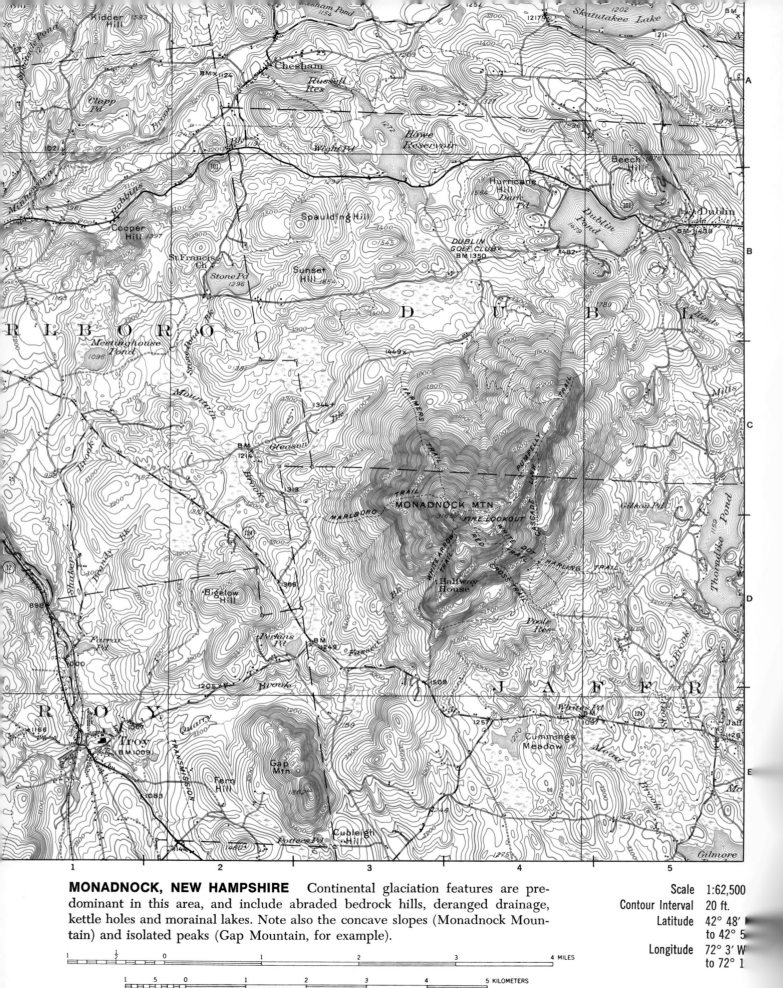

MONADNOCK, NEW HAMPSHIRE Continental glaciation features are predominant in this area, and include abraded bedrock hills, deranged drainage, kettle holes and morainal lakes. Note also the concave slopes (Monadnock Mountain) and isolated peaks (Gap Mountain, for example).

Scale 1:62,500
Contour Interval 20 ft.
Latitude 42° 48′
to 42° 5
Longitude 72° 3′ W
to 72° 1

1   ½   0   1   2   3   4 MILES

1   5   0   1   2   3   4   5 KILOMETERS

62

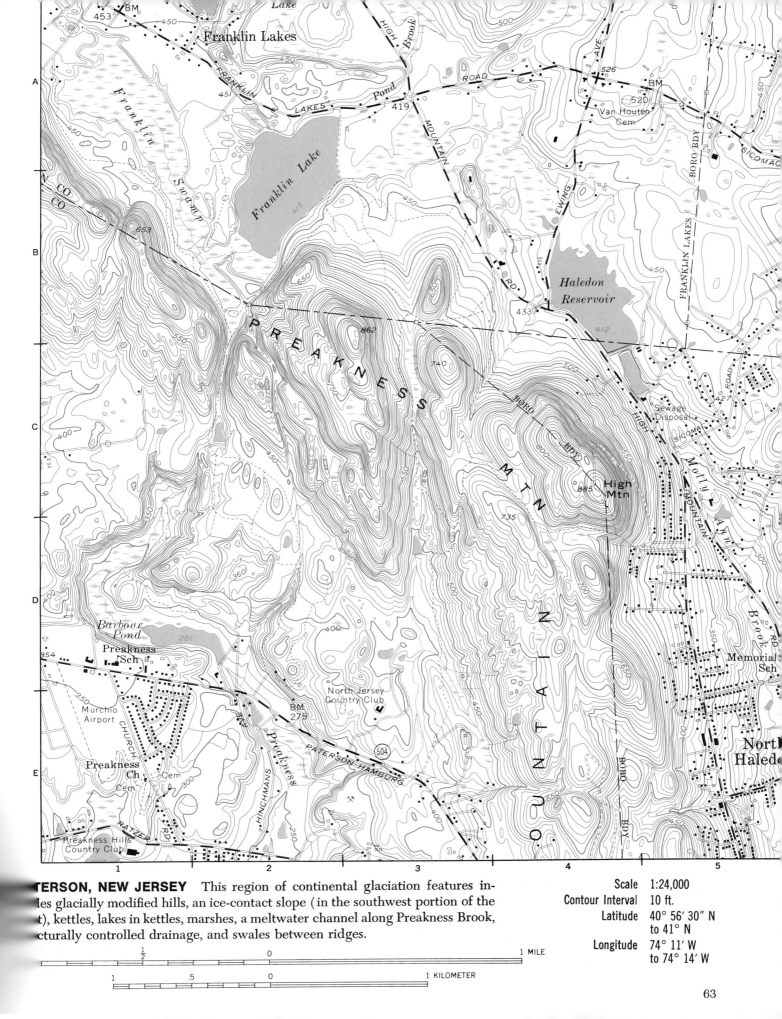

TERSON, NEW JERSEY This region of continental glaciation features includes glacially modified hills, an ice-contact slope (in the southwest portion of the
t), kettles, lakes in kettles, marshes, a meltwater channel along Preakness Brook,
cturally controlled drainage, and swales between ridges.

Scale 1:24,000
Contour Interval 10 ft.
Latitude 40° 56′ 30″ N
to 41° N
Longitude 74° 11′ W
to 74° 14′ W

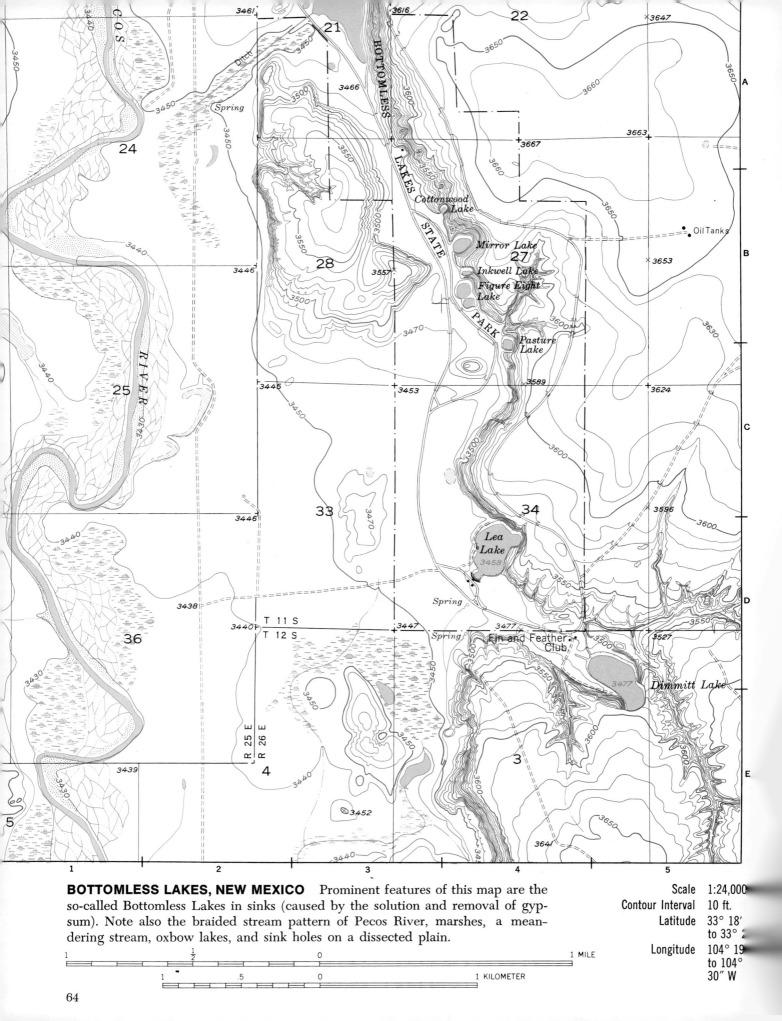

BOTTOMLESS LAKES, NEW MEXICO Prominent features of this map are the so-called Bottomless Lakes in sinks (caused by the solution and removal of gypsum). Note also the braided stream pattern of Pecos River, marshes, a meandering stream, oxbow lakes, and sink holes on a dissected plain.

Scale   1:24,000

Contour Interval   10 ft.

Latitude   33° 18′
to 33°

Longitude   104° 19′
to 104°
30″ W

1 MILE

1 KILOMETER

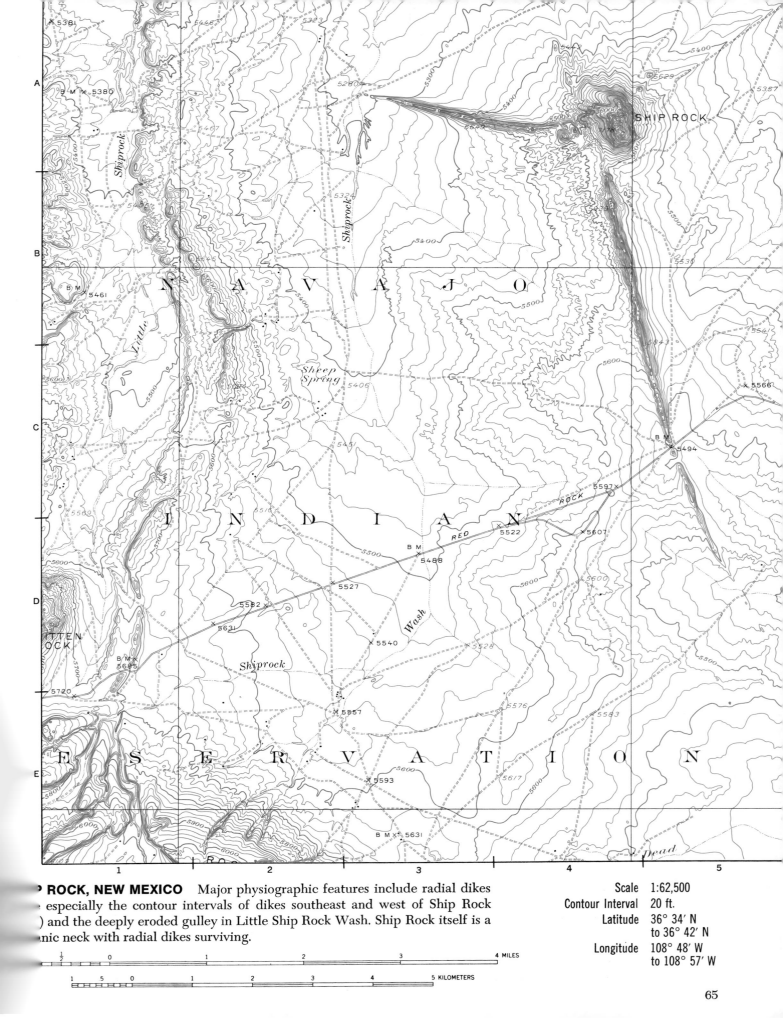

ROCK, NEW MEXICO Major physiographic features include radial dikes
especially the contour intervals of dikes southeast and west of Ship Rock
and the deeply eroded gulley in Little Ship Rock Wash. Ship Rock itself is a
nic neck with radial dikes surviving.

Scale 1:62,500
Contour Interval 20 ft.
Latitude 36° 34′ N
to 36° 42′ N
Longitude 108° 48′ W
to 108° 57′ W

AMSTERDAM, NEW YORK Physiographic features of this continental glaciation area include a dissected glaciated plateau, kames, river bluffs along the Mohawk River, and a U-shaped valley with terraced banks. Note also the abandoned Erie Canal in the river channel (including locks).

Scale 1:62,50[
Contour Interval 20 ft.
Latitude 42° 46
to 42°
Longitude 74° W
to 74°

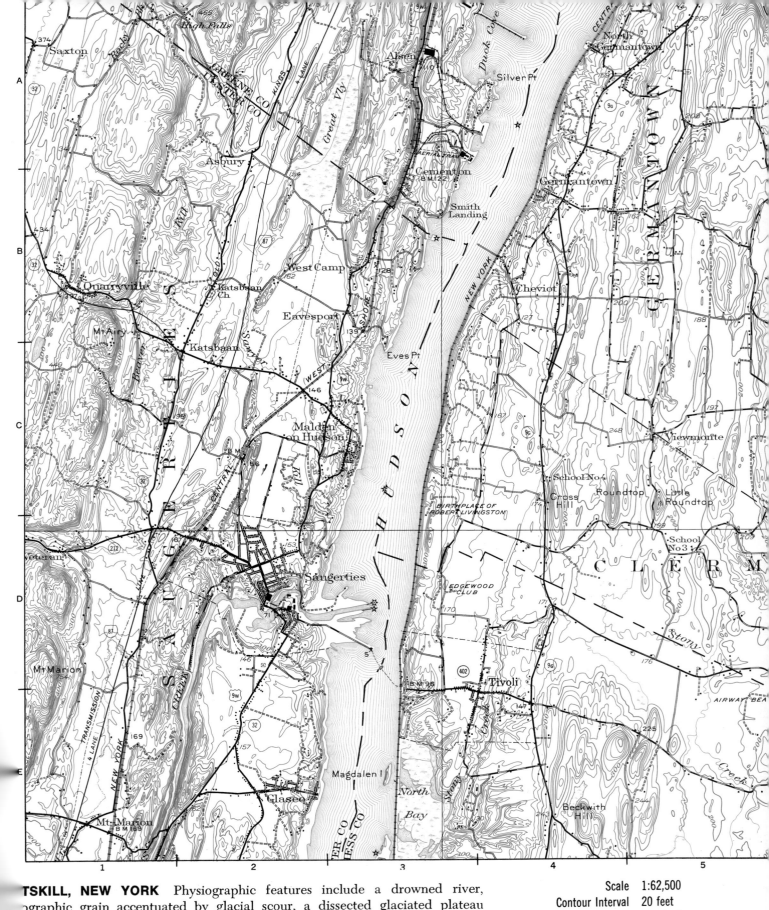

CATSKILL, NEW YORK Physiographic features include a drowned river, topographic grain accentuated by glacial scour, a dissected glaciated plateau bounded on the east by an escarpment, drumlins, dendritic drainage, reverse drainage, limestone quarries, and ridges.

Scale	1:62,500
Contour Interval	20 feet
Latitude	42° 3′ N to 42° 10′ N
Longitude	73° 51′ W to 74° W

4 MILES

5 KILOMETERS

67

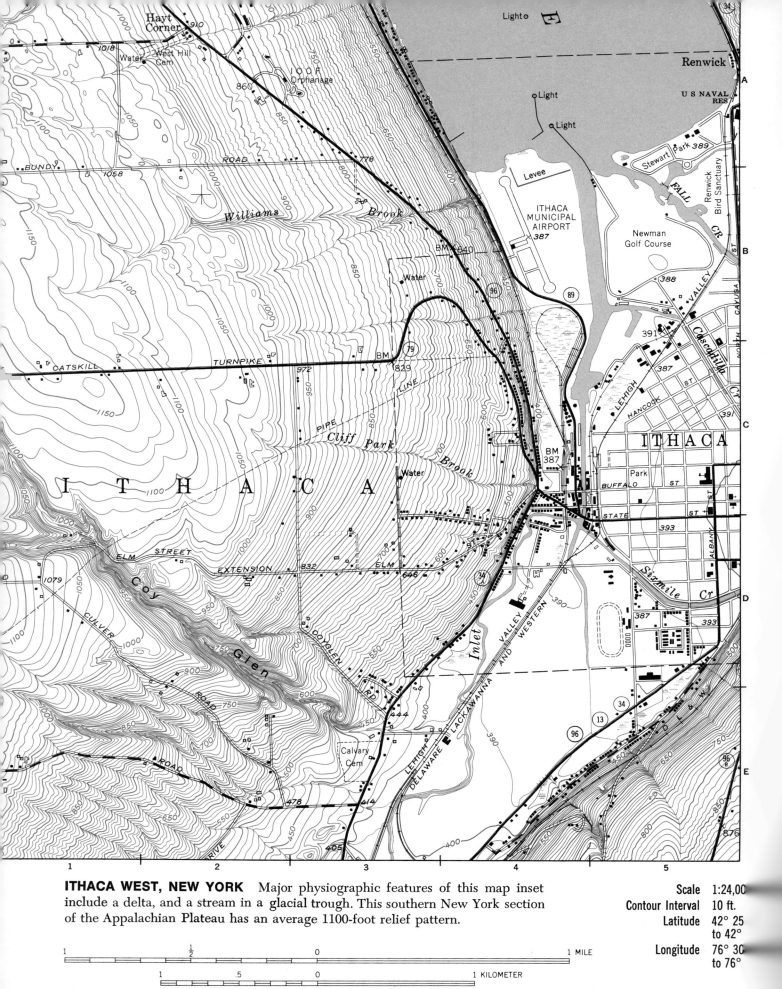

ITHACA WEST, NEW YORK Major physiographic features of this map inset include a delta, and a stream in a glacial trough. This southern New York section of the Appalachian Plateau has an average 1100-foot relief pattern.

Scale   1:24,00

Contour Interval   10 ft.

Latitude   42° 25 to 42°

Longitude   76° 30 to 76°

1   ½   0   1 MILE

1   .5   0   1 KILOMETER

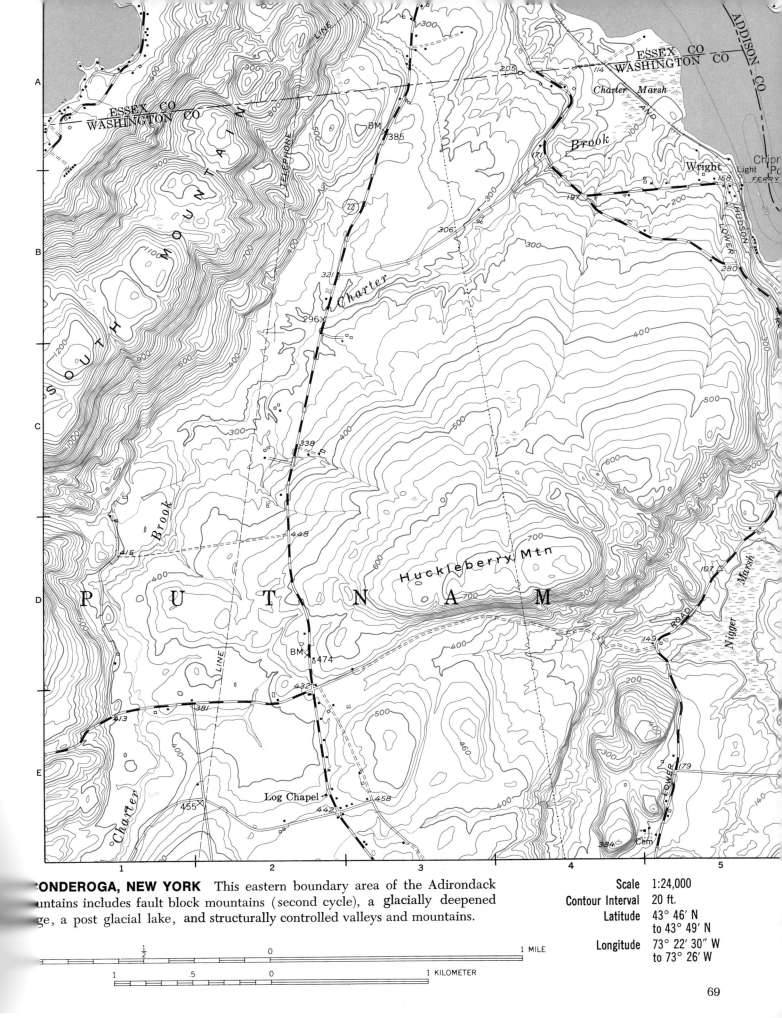

ICONDEROGA, NEW YORK This eastern boundary area of the Adirondack untains includes fault block mountains (second cycle), a glacially deepened ge, a post glacial lake, and structurally controlled valleys and mountains.

Scale 1:24,000
Contour Interval 20 ft.
Latitude 43° 46′ N
to 43° 49′ N
Longitude 73° 22′ 30″ W
to 73° 26′ W

½   0   1 MILE

1   .5   0   1 KILOMETER

69

MOUNT MITCHELL, NORTH CAROLINA Physiographic features include the Blue Ridge Front with erosional escarpment, Mount Mitchell (highest elevation in eastern United States), subcontinental divide between the Gulf of Mexico and the Atlantic Ocean, and a dissected mountainous highland.

Scale 1:125,00

Contour Interval 100 ft.

Latitude 35° 37'
to 35°

Longitude 82° 7'
to 82°

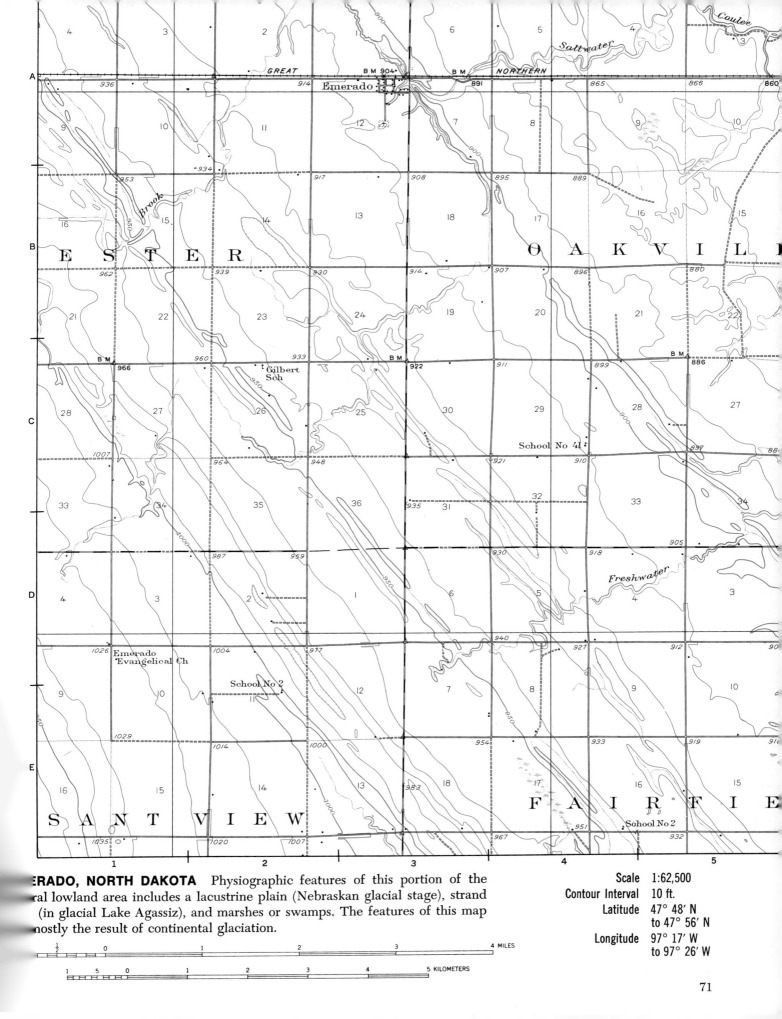

ERADO, NORTH DAKOTA Physiographic features of this portion of the ral lowland area includes a lacustrine plain (Nebraskan glacial stage), strand (in glacial Lake Agassiz), and marshes or swamps. The features of this map nostly the result of continental glaciation.

Scale 1:62,500
Contour Interval 10 ft.
Latitude 47° 48′ N
to 47° 56′ N
Longitude 97° 17′ W
to 97° 26′ W

4 MILES

5 KILOMETERS

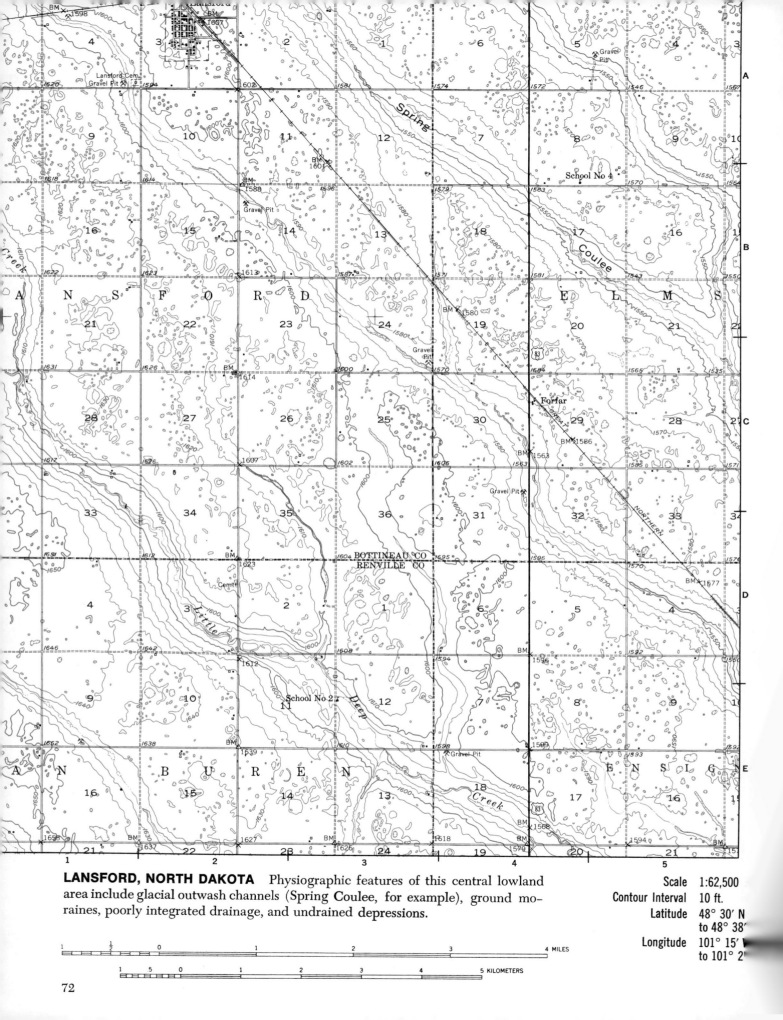

LANSFORD, NORTH DAKOTA Physiographic features of this central lowland area include glacial outwash channels (Spring Coulee, for example), ground moraines, poorly integrated drainage, and undrained depressions.

Scale 1:62,500
Contour Interval 10 ft.
Latitude 48° 30′ N
to 48° 38′
Longitude 101° 15′
to 101° 2

1 MILES

5 KILOMETERS

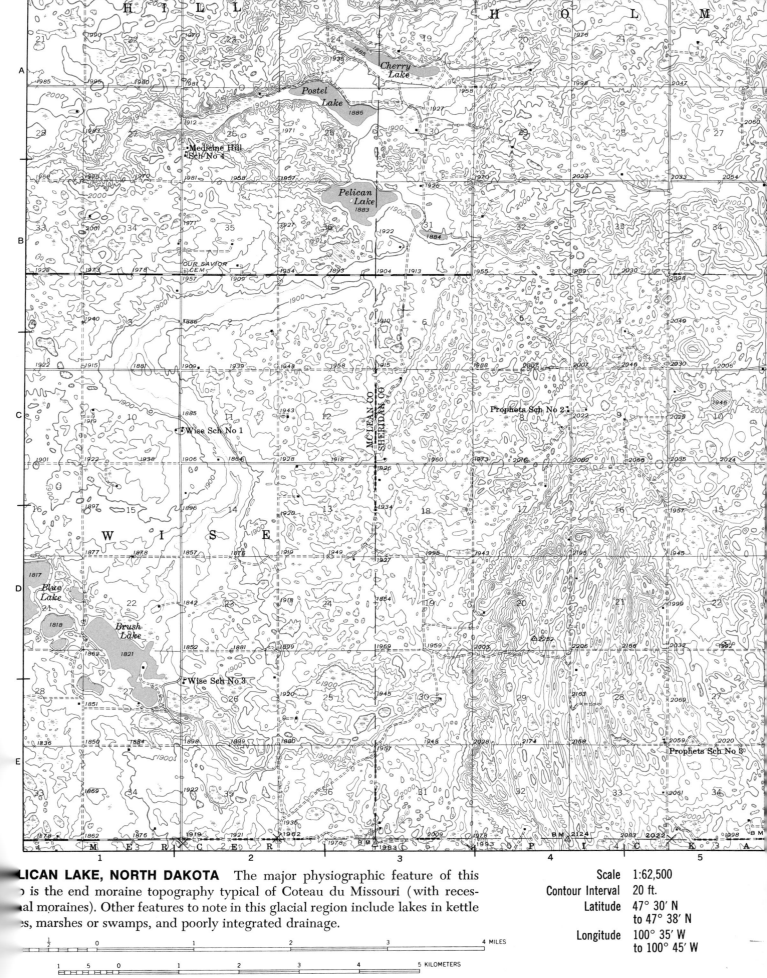

PELICAN LAKE, NORTH DAKOTA The major physiographic feature of this map is the end moraine topography typical of Coteau du Missouri (with recessional moraines). Other features to note in this glacial region include lakes in kettle holes, marshes or swamps, and poorly integrated drainage.

Scale 1:62,500

Contour Interval 20 ft.

Latitude 47° 30′ N to 47° 38′ N

Longitude 100° 35′ W to 100° 45′ W

½ 0 1 2 3 4 MILES

1 5 0 1 2 3 4 5 KILOMETERS

73

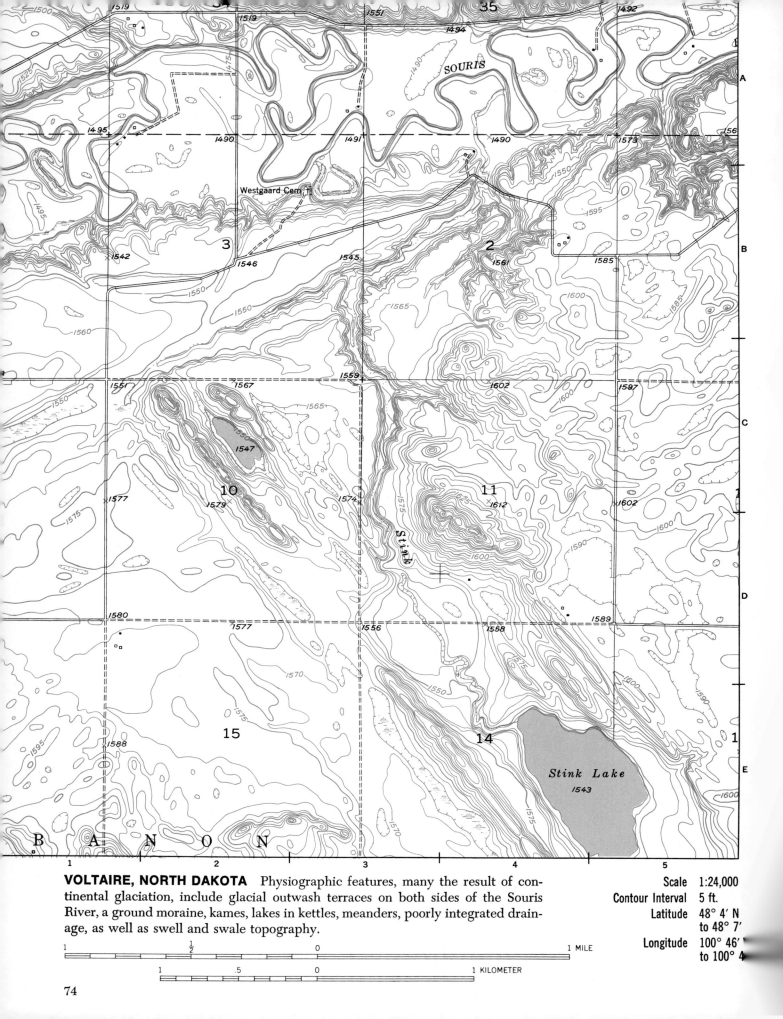

VOLTAIRE, NORTH DAKOTA Physiographic features, many the result of continental glaciation, include glacial outwash terraces on both sides of the Souris River, a ground moraine, kames, lakes in kettles, meanders, poorly integrated drainage, as well as swell and swale topography.

Scale 1:24,000
Contour Interval 5 ft.
Latitude 48° 4′ N
to 48° 7′
Longitude 100° 46′
to 100° 4

1 MILE

1 KILOMETER

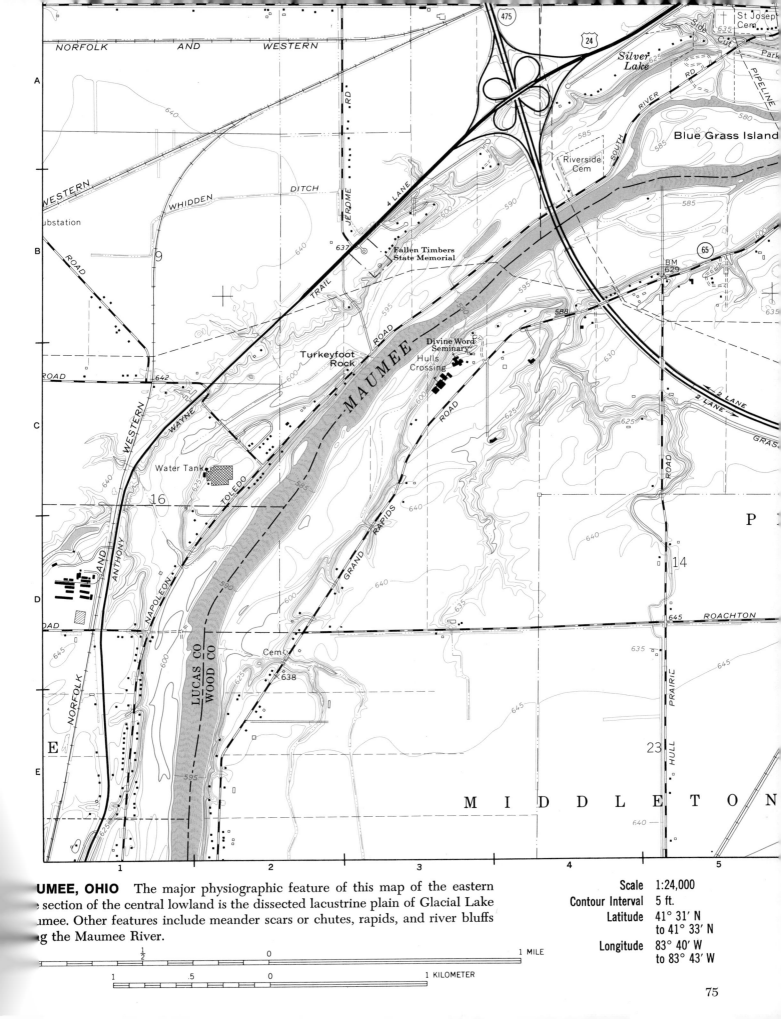

MAUMEE, OHIO The major physiographic feature of this map of the eastern section of the central lowland is the dissected lacustrine plain of Glacial Lake Maumee. Other features include meander scars or chutes, rapids, and river bluffs along the Maumee River.

Scale 1:24,000
Contour Interval 5 ft.
Latitude 41° 31' N
to 41° 33' N
Longitude 83° 40' W
to 83° 43' W

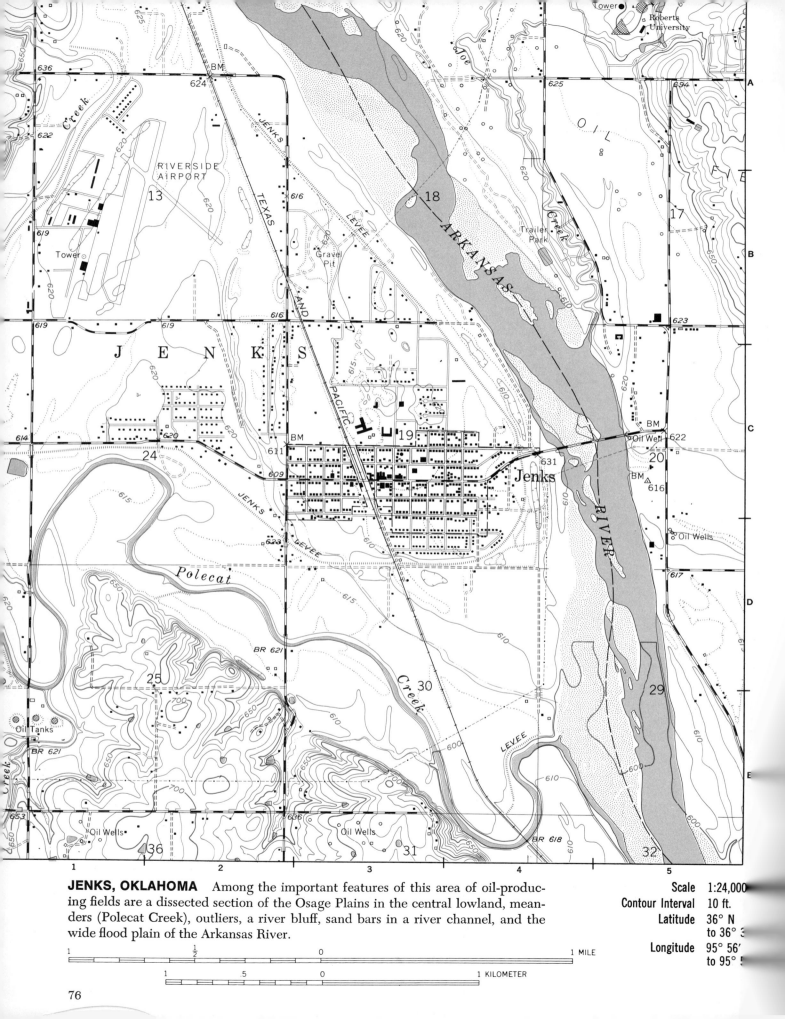

JENKS, OKLAHOMA Among the important features of this area of oil-producing fields are a dissected section of the Osage Plains in the central lowland, meanders (Polecat Creek), outliers, a river bluff, sand bars in a river channel, and the wide flood plain of the Arkansas River.

Scale 1:24,000
Contour Interval 10 ft.
Latitude 36° N
to 36° 3
Longitude 95° 56'
to 95° 5

1 MILE

1 KILOMETER

NDON, OREGON Physiographic features include a diverted outlet (Coquille er), a marine terrace, prograded shore, beach ridges uplifted and modified by dunes, a point (Coquille), sea stacks, tidal marshes, wave-cut cliffs, and s.

Scale 1:62,500
Contour Interval 50 ft.
Latitude 43° 5′ N
to 43° 13′ N
Longitude 124° 17′ W
to 124° 27′ W

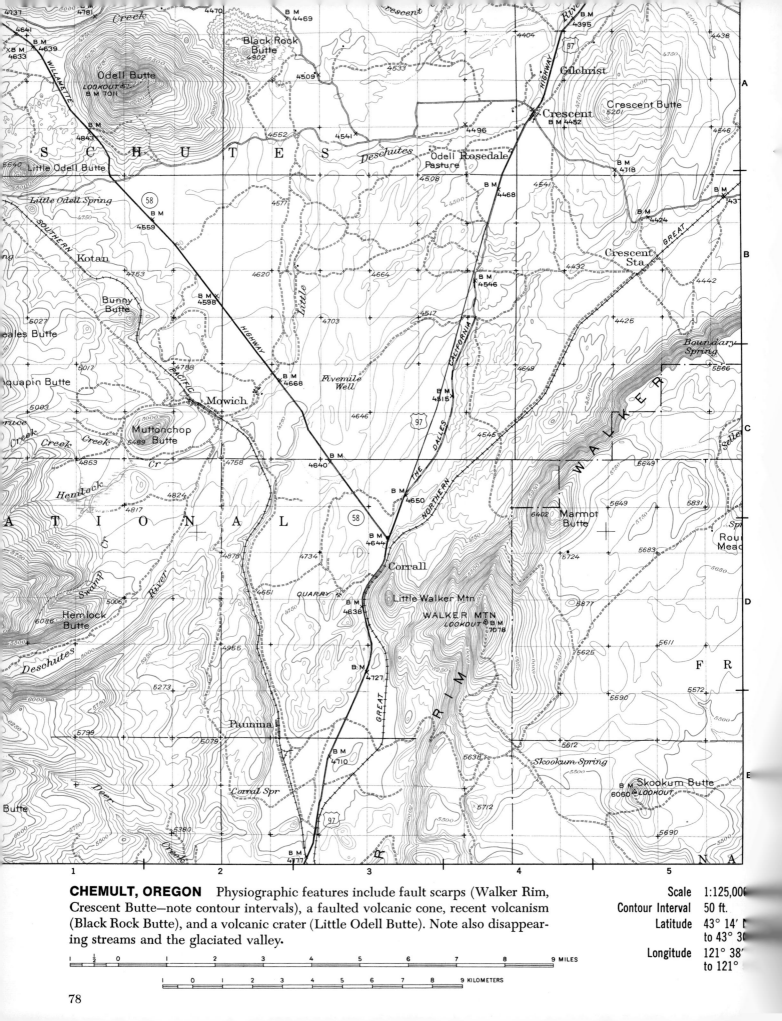

CHEMULT, OREGON Physiographic features include fault scarps (Walker Rim, Crescent Butte—note contour intervals), a faulted volcanic cone, recent volcanism (Black Rock Butte), and a volcanic crater (Little Odell Butte). Note also disappearing streams and the glaciated valley.

Scale 1:125,000

Contour Interval 50 ft.

Latitude 43° 14′ to 43° 30′

Longitude 121° 38′ to 121°

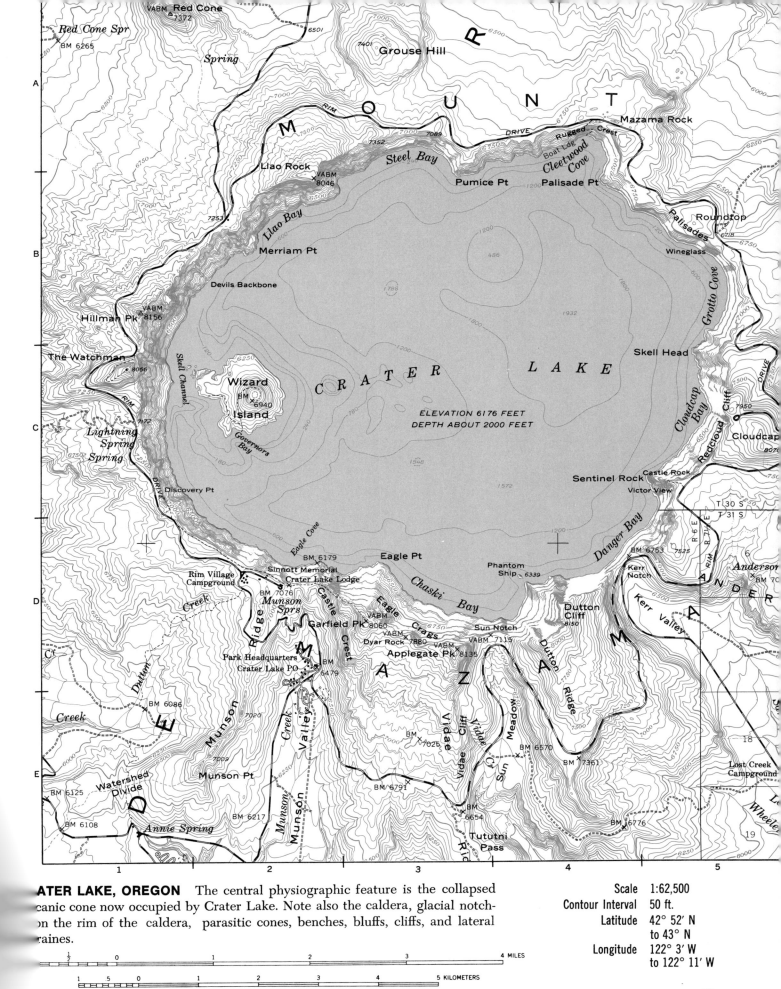

CRATER LAKE, OREGON The central physiographic feature is the collapsed volcanic cone now occupied by Crater Lake. Note also the caldera, glacial notches on the rim of the caldera, parasitic cones, benches, bluffs, cliffs, and lateral moraines.

Scale	1:62,500
Contour Interval	50 ft.
Latitude	42° 52′ N
	to 43° N
Longitude	122° 3′ W
	to 122° 11′ W

GALICE, OREGON An important feature of this map is the old high level channel of the Rogue River with placer deposits. Other features include the Rogue River canyon, a dissected upland, entrenched meanders, terraces, and a V-shaped valley.

Scale 1:62,500
Contour Interval 50 ft.
Latitude 42° 30′ to 42° 3
Longitude 123° 32 to 123°

1   ½   0   1   2   3   4 MILES

1   5   0   1   2   3   4   5 KILOMETERS

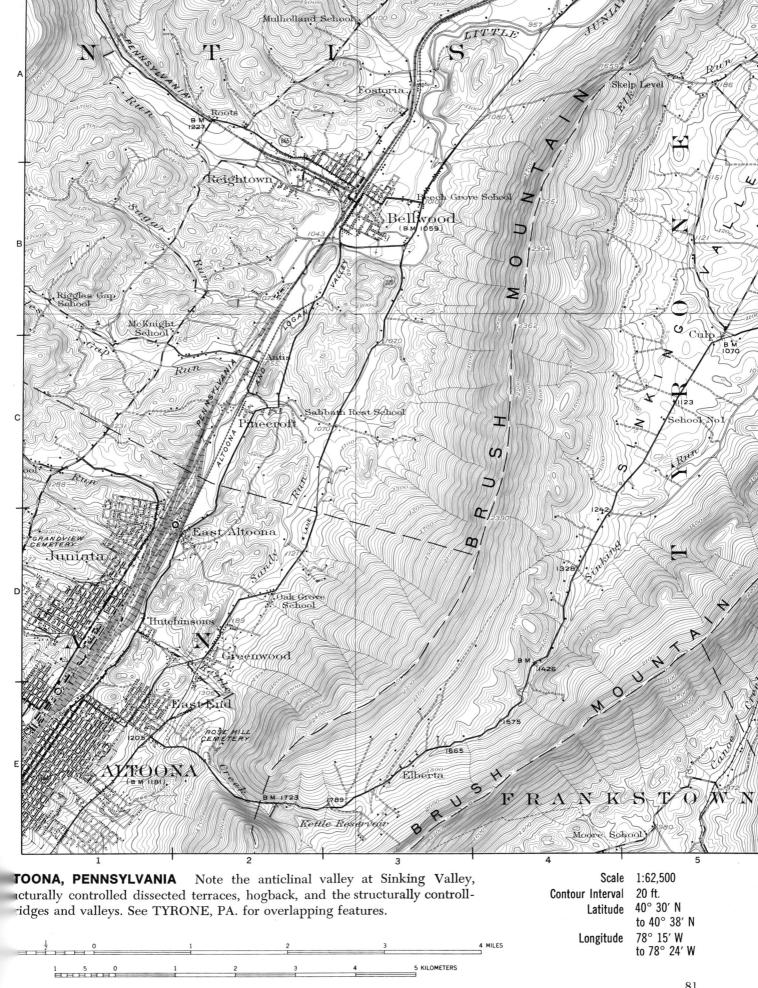

TOONA, PENNSYLVANIA   Note the anticlinal valley at Sinking Valley, ...cturally controlled dissected terraces, hogback, and the structurally controll- ...ridges and valleys. See TYRONE, PA. for overlapping features.

Scale	1:62,500
Contour Interval	20 ft.
Latitude	40° 30′ N
	to 40° 38′ N
Longitude	78° 15′ W
	to 78° 24′ W

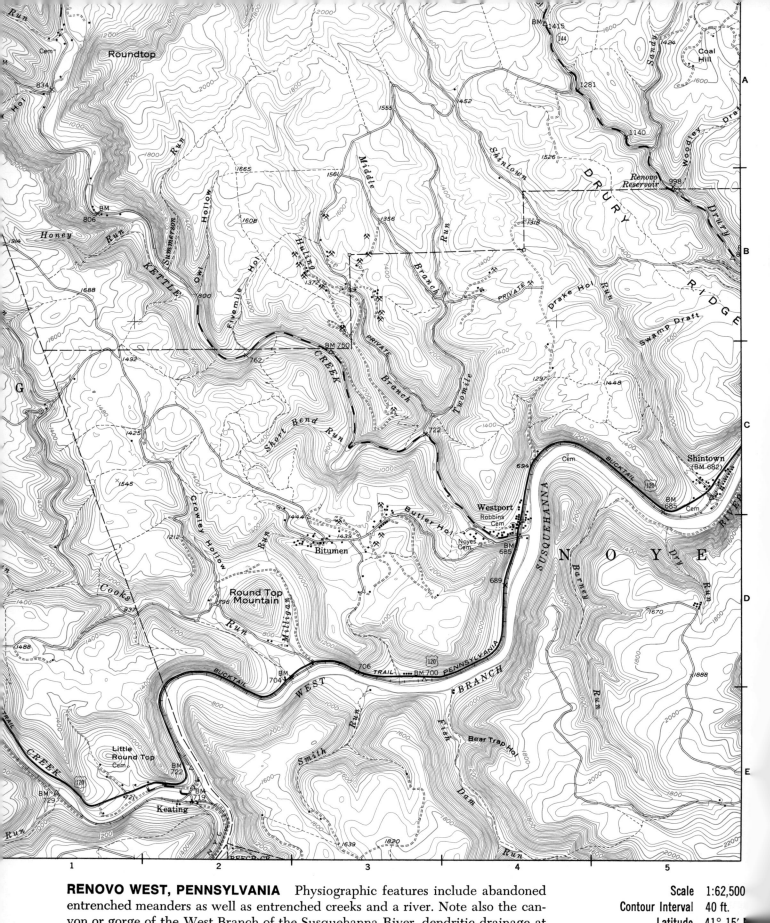

RENOVO WEST, PENNSYLVANIA Physiographic features include abandoned entrenched meanders as well as entrenched creeks and a river. Note also the canyon or gorge of the West Branch of the Susquehanna River, dendritic drainage at Drury Run, and meander cores of Round Top and Little Round Top Mountains.

Scale 1:62,500
Contour Interval 40 ft.
Latitude 41° 15′
to 41° 2
Longitude 77° 48′
to 77° 5

1 ½ 0 1 2 3 4 MILES

1 .5 0 1 2 3 4 5 KILOMETERS

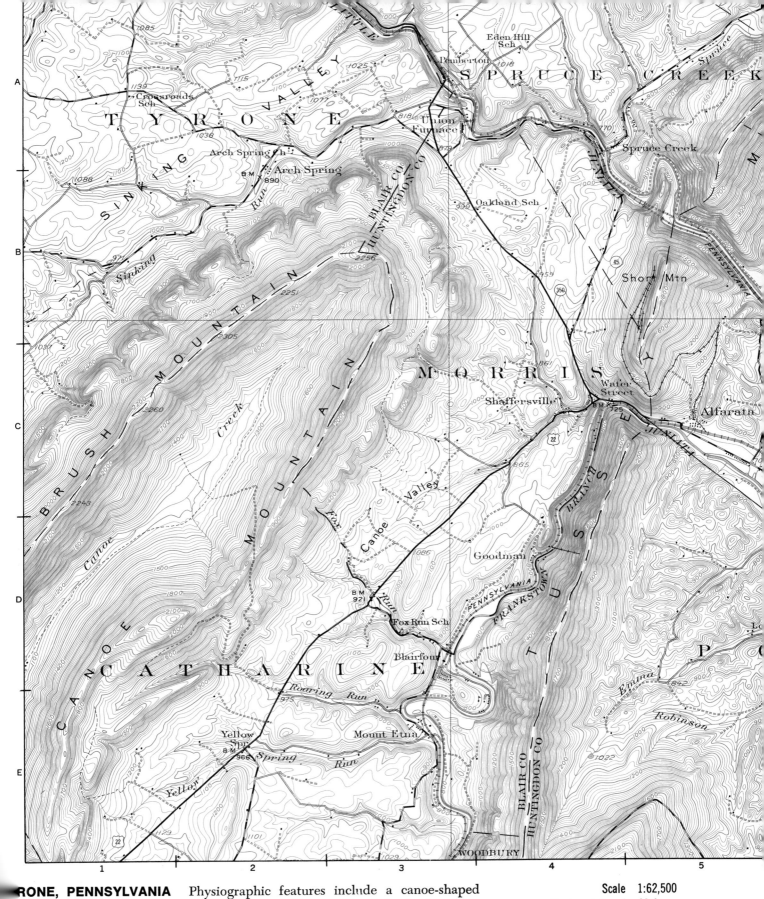

RONE, PENNSYLVANIA Physiographic features include a canoe-shaped ~~un~~tain, a dissected plateau, entrenched stream (Juniata River), hogbacks, struc-~~a~~lly controlled dissected terraces, a synclinal valley and mountain, and water ~~s~~. See ALTOONA, PA. for overlapping features.

Scale	1:62,500
Contour Interval	20 ft.
Latitude	40° 30' N to 40° 38' N
Longitude	78° 7' W to 78° 15' W

4 MILES

5 KILOMETERS

83

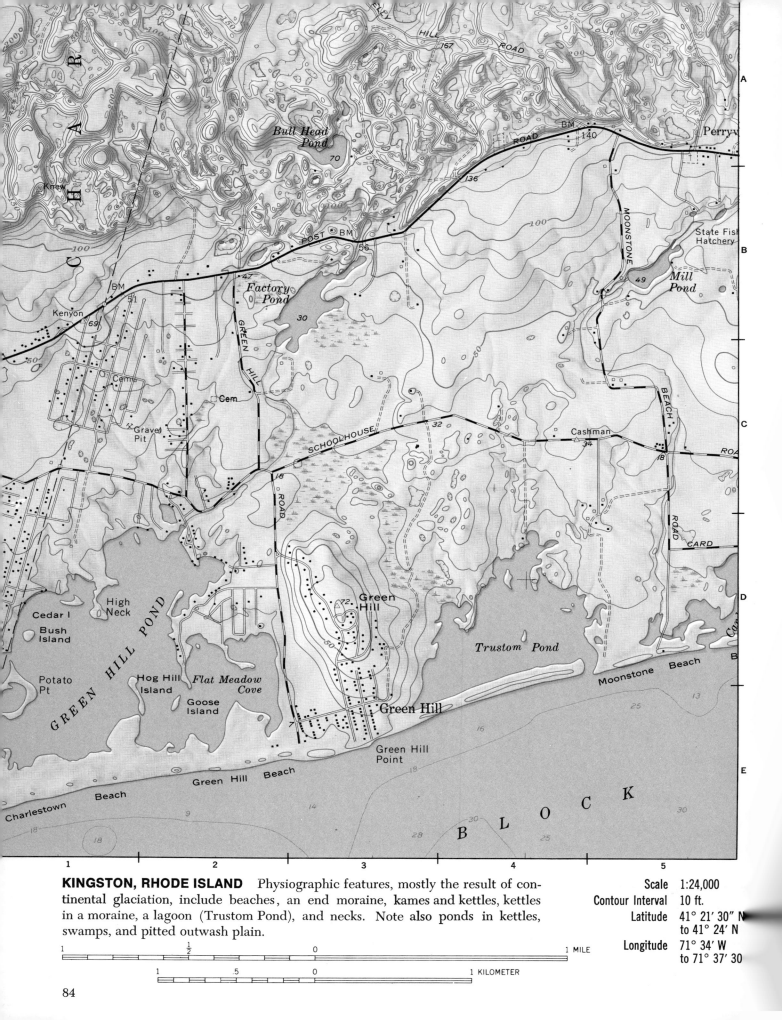

KINGSTON, RHODE ISLAND Physiographic features, mostly the result of continental glaciation, include beaches, an end moraine, kames and kettles, kettles in a moraine, a lagoon (Trustom Pond), and necks. Note also ponds in kettles, swamps, and pitted outwash plain.

Scale 1:24,000
Contour Interval 10 ft.
Latitude 41° 21′ 30″ N
to 41° 24′ N
Longitude 71° 34′ W
to 71° 37′ 30″

1 ½ 0 1 MILE

1 .5 0 1 KILOMETER

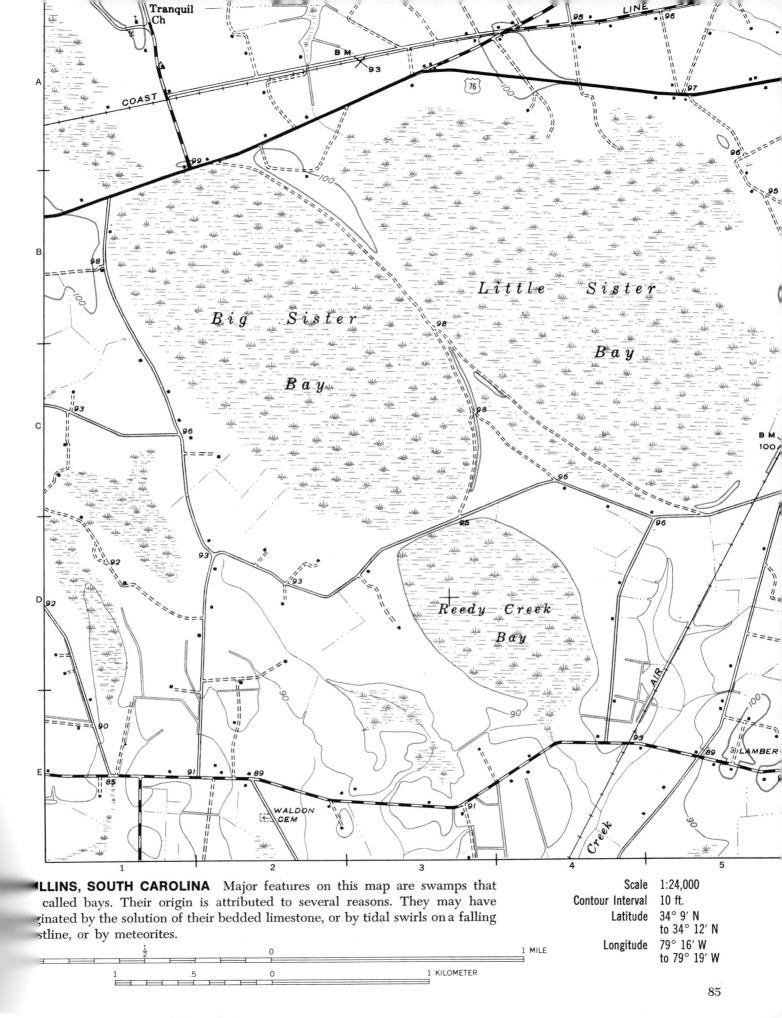

Tranquil
Ch

COAST

LINE

95   96

BM
93

76

100   97

99

100

98   96

100

95

Little   Sister

Big   Sister   98

Bay

98

Bay

93

96

98

BM
100

96

92

96

95

93

96

93

92   *Reedy Creek*

93   *Bay*

90

AIR

90   100

90

93   89   LAMBER

90   89

91

85

90

91

85   WALDON
CEM

91

90

Creek

1   2   3   4   5

A

B

C

D

E

LLINS, SOUTH CAROLINA Major features on this map are swamps that
called bays. Their origin is attributed to several reasons. They may have
ginated by the solution of their bedded limestone, or by tidal swirls on a falling
stline, or by meteorites.

Scale   1:24,000
Contour Interval   10 ft.
Latitude   34° 9' N
to 34° 12' N
Longitude   79° 16' W
to 79° 19' W

½   0   1 MILE

1   .5   0   1 KILOMETER

85

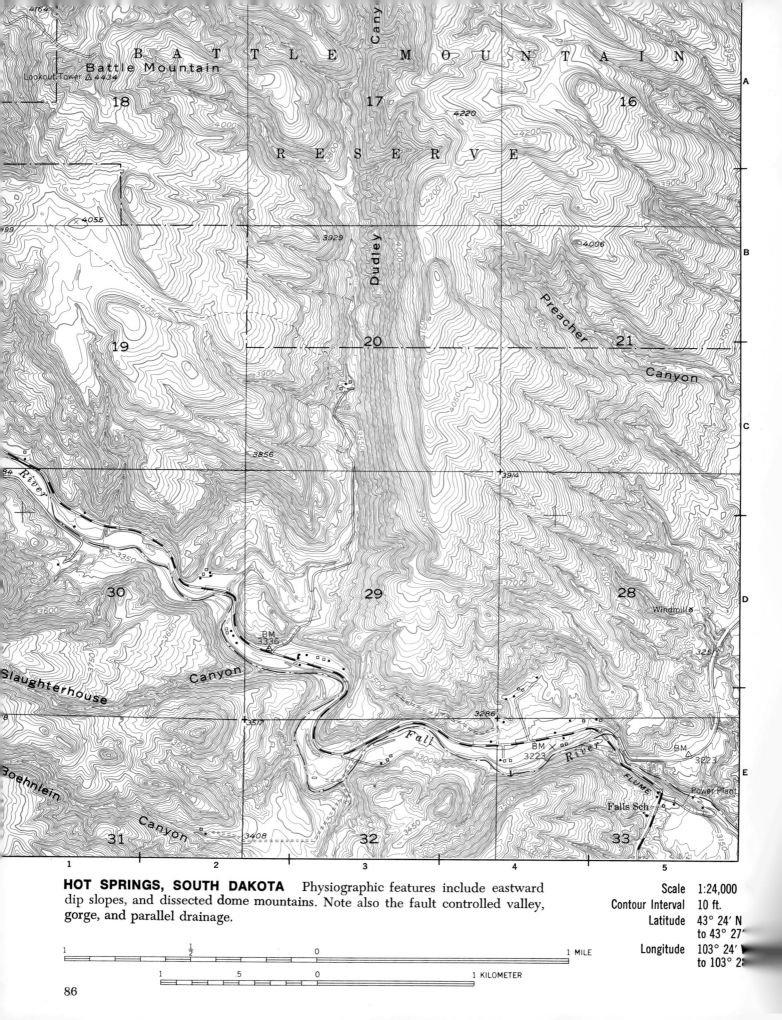

HOT SPRINGS, SOUTH DAKOTA Physiographic features include eastward
dip slopes, and dissected dome mountains. Note also the fault controlled valley,
gorge, and parallel drainage.

Scale 1:24,000
Contour Interval 10 ft.
Latitude 43° 24′ N
to 43° 27′
Longitude 103° 24′
to 103° 2

1   ½   0   1 MILE

1   .5   0   1 KILOMETER

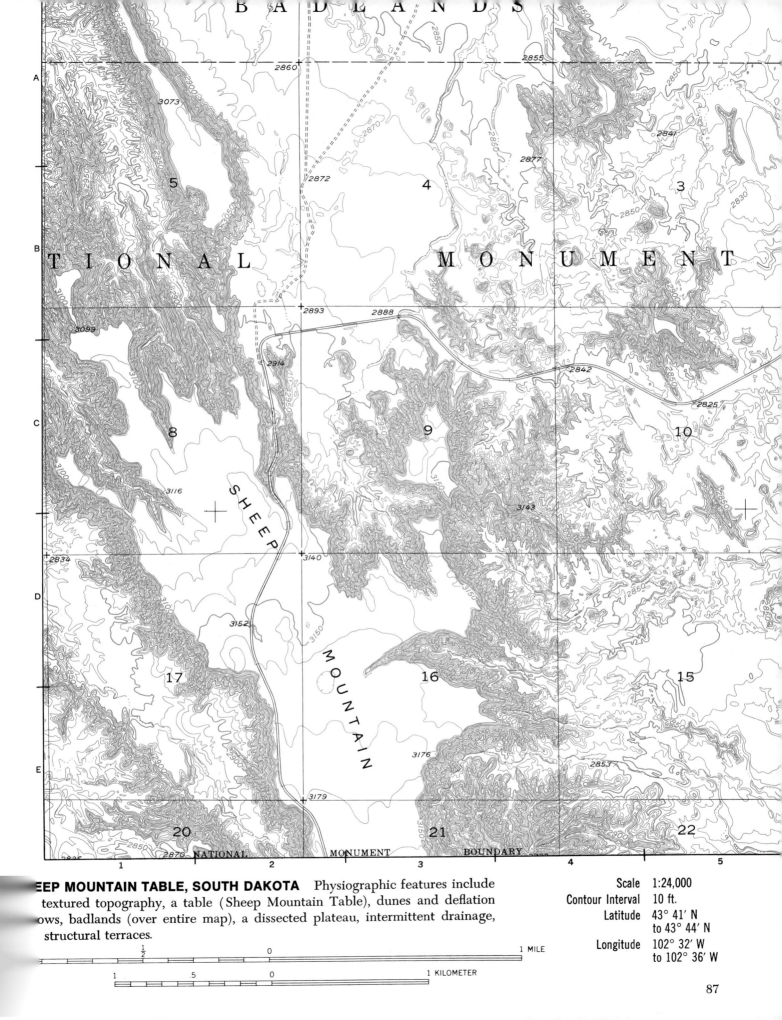

EEP MOUNTAIN TABLE, SOUTH DAKOTA Physiographic features include textured topography, a table (Sheep Mountain Table), dunes and deflation ws, badlands (over entire map), a dissected plateau, intermittent drainage, structural terraces.

Scale 1:24,000
Contour Interval 10 ft.
Latitude 43° 41′ N
to 43° 44′ N
Longitude 102° 32′ W
to 102° 36′ W

½   0   1 MILE

1   .5   0   1 KILOMETER

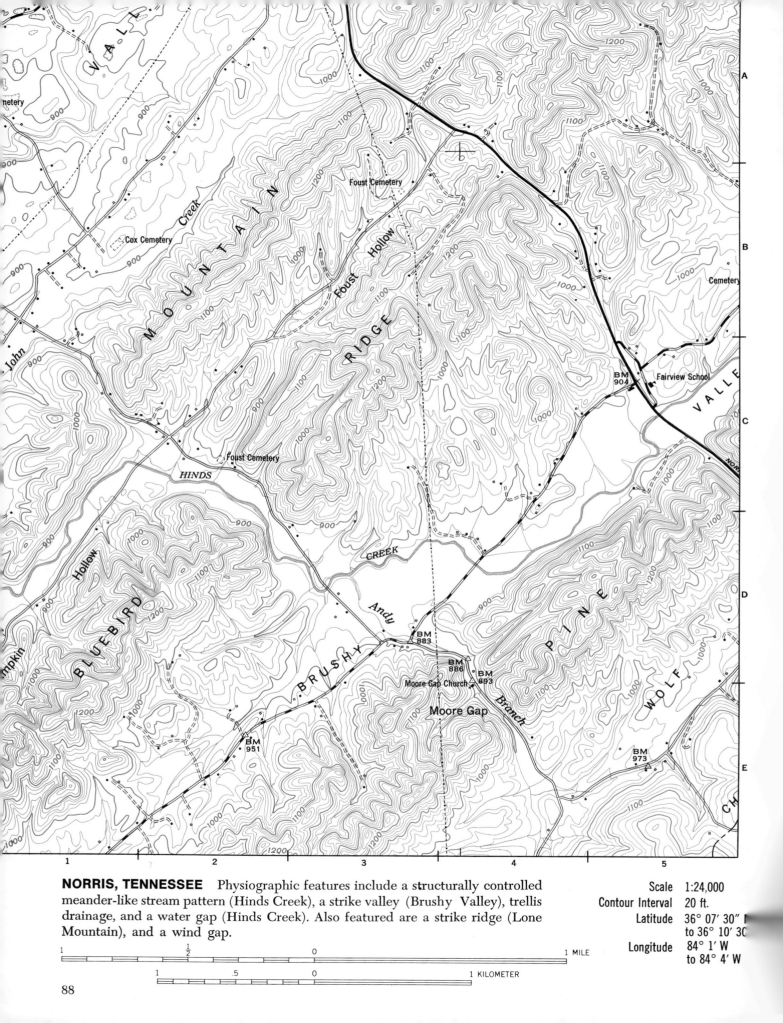

NORRIS, TENNESSEE Physiographic features include a structurally controlled meander-like stream pattern (Hinds Creek), a strike valley (Brushy Valley), trellis drainage, and a water gap (Hinds Creek). Also featured are a strike ridge (Lone Mountain), and a wind gap.

Scale 1:24,000
Contour Interval 20 ft.
Latitude 36° 07′ 30″
to 36° 10′ 30
Longitude 84° 1′ W
to 84° 4′ W

1 MILE

1 KILOMETER

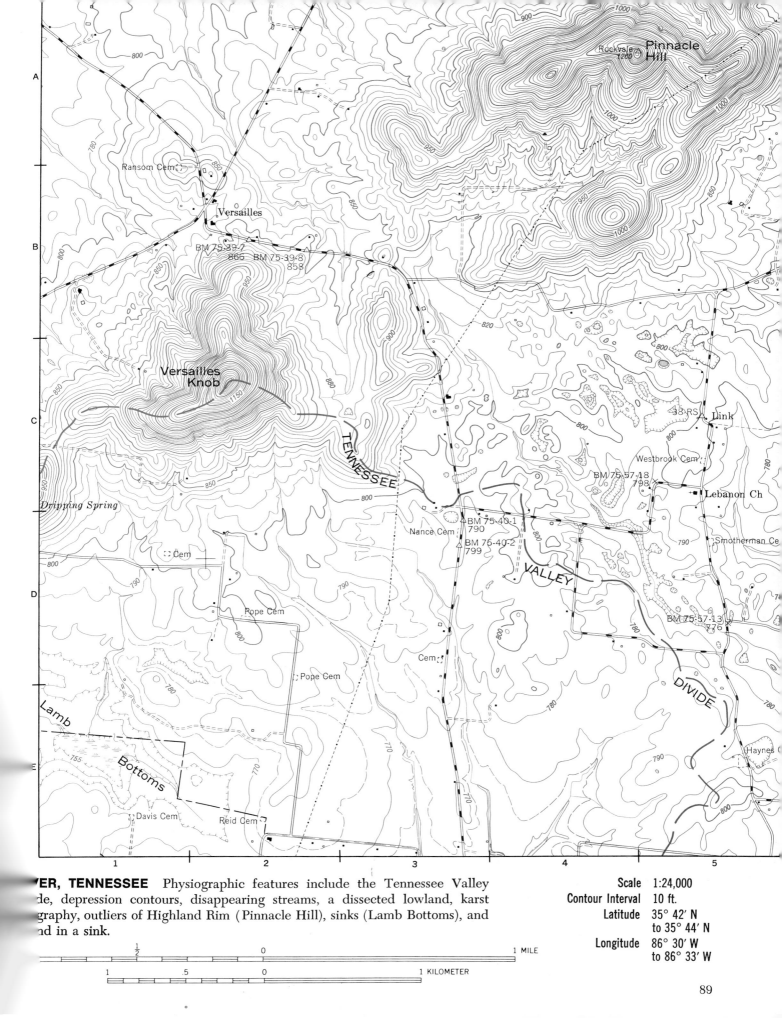

Rockvale
1260
Pinnacle Hill
Ransom Cem
Versailles
BM 75-39-7
866
BM 75-39-8
858
Versailles Knob
1150
TENNESSEE
VALLEY
DIVIDE
Dripping Spring
Nance Cem
BM 75-40-1
790
BM 75-40-2
799
Cem
Pope Cem
Pope Cem
Cem
Lamb
Bottoms
755
Davis Cem
Reid Cem
38 RS
Link
Westbrook Cem
BM 75-57-18
798
Lebanon Ch
Smotherman Ce
BM 75-57-13
776
Haynes
800
820
850
900
950
1000
780
790
770
A
B
C
D
E
1
2
3
4
5

ʼER, TENNESSEE Physiographic features include the Tennessee Valley de, depression contours, disappearing streams, a dissected lowland, karst graphy, outliers of Highland Rim (Pinnacle Hill), sinks (Lamb Bottoms), and nd in a sink.

½ 0 1 MILE

1 .5 0 1 KILOMETER

Scale	1:24,000
Contour Interval	10 ft.
Latitude	35° 42′ N to 35° 44′ N
Longitude	86° 30′ W to 86° 33′ W

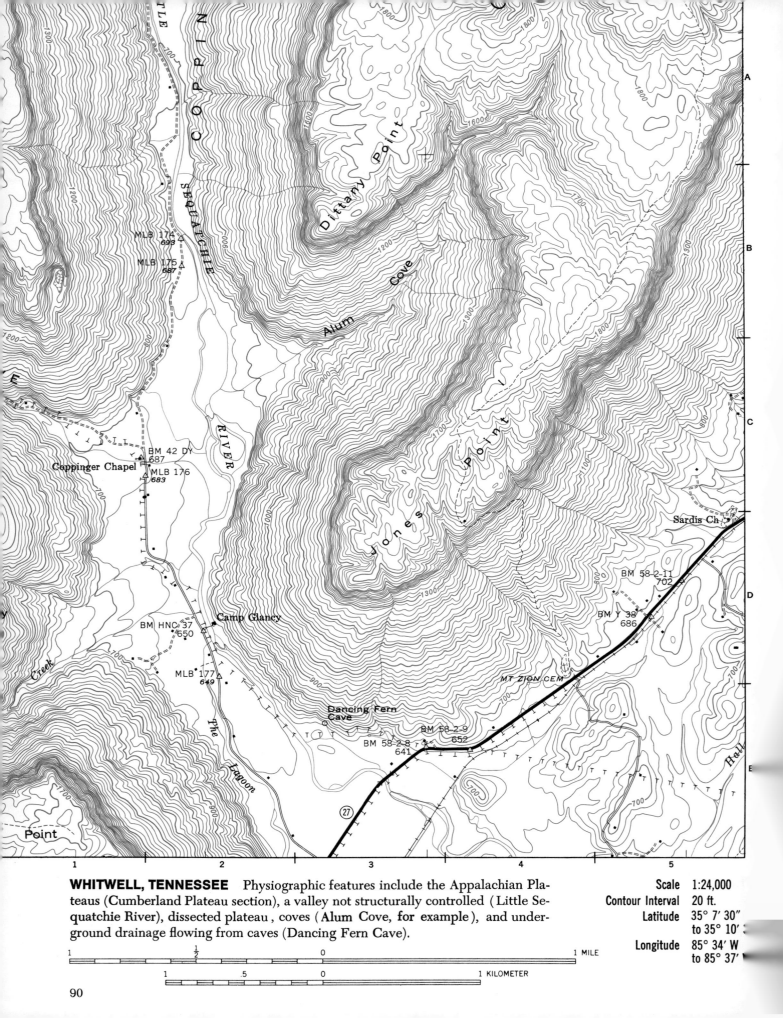

WHITWELL, TENNESSEE Physiographic features include the Appalachian Plateaus (Cumberland Plateau section), a valley not structurally controlled (Little Sequatchie River), dissected plateau, coves (**Alum Cove**, for example), and underground drainage flowing from caves (Dancing Fern Cave).

Scale	1:24,000
Contour Interval	20 ft.
Latitude	35° 7′ 30″
	to 35° 10′
Longitude	85° 34′ W
	to 85° 37′

1   ½   0   1 MILE

1   .5   0   1 KILOMETER

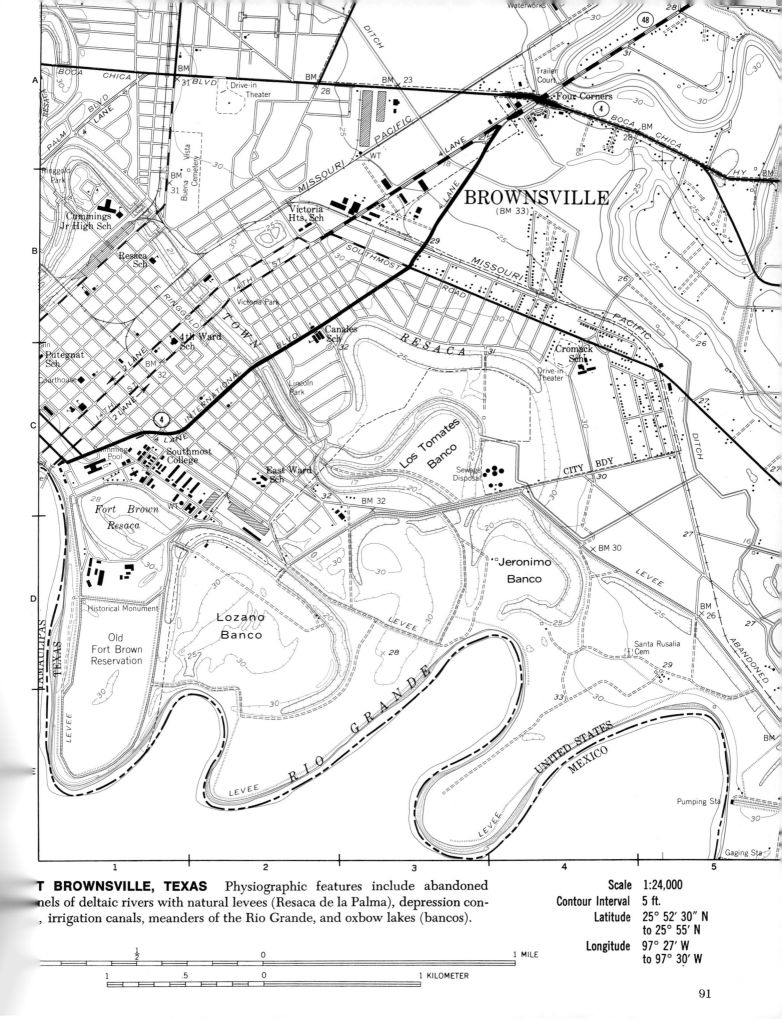

BROWNSVILLE

(BM 33)

BROWNSVILLE, TEXAS Physiographic features include abandoned nels of deltaic rivers with natural levees (Resaca de la Palma), depression con-, irrigation canals, meanders of the Rio Grande, and oxbow lakes (bancos).

Scale 1:24,000
Contour Interval 5 ft.
Latitude 25° 52′ 30″ N
to 25° 55′ N
Longitude 97° 27′ W
to 97° 30′ W

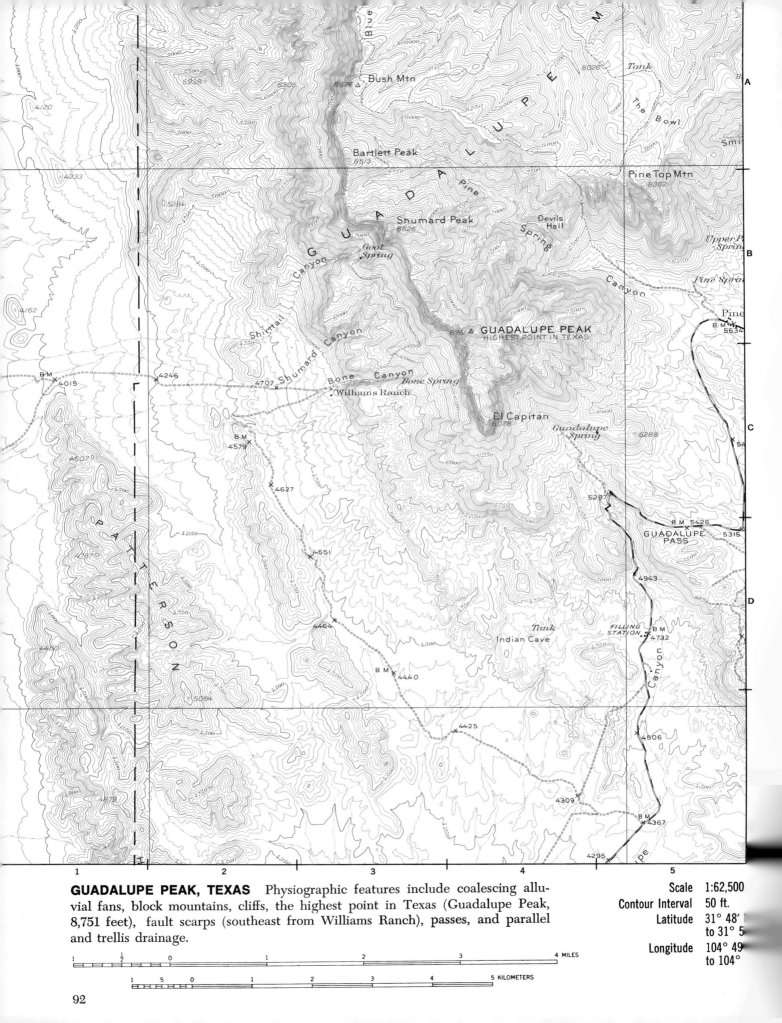

GUADALUPE PEAK, TEXAS Physiographic features include coalescing alluvial fans, block mountains, cliffs, the highest point in Texas (Guadalupe Peak, 8,751 feet), fault scarps (southeast from Williams Ranch), passes, and parallel and trellis drainage.

Scale 1:62,500
Contour Interval 50 ft.
Latitude 31° 48′ to 31° 5
Longitude 104° 49 to 104°

1   ½   0   1   2   3   4 MILES

1 5 0   1   2   3   4   5 KILOMETERS

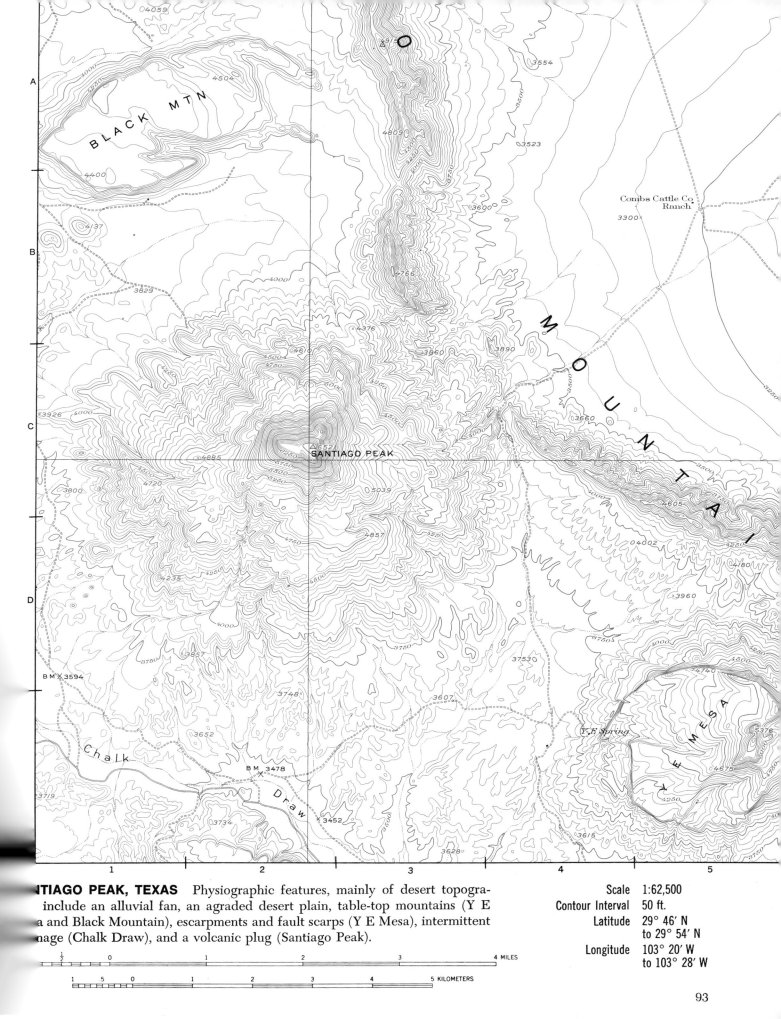

SANTIAGO PEAK, TEXAS Physiographic features, mainly of desert topography, include an alluvial fan, an agraded desert plain, table-top mountains (Y E Mesa and Black Mountain), escarpments and fault scarps (Y E Mesa), intermittent drainage (Chalk Draw), and a volcanic plug (Santiago Peak).

Scale 1:62,500
Contour Interval 50 ft.
Latitude 29° 46′ N
to 29° 54′ N
Longitude 103° 20′ W
to 103° 28′ W

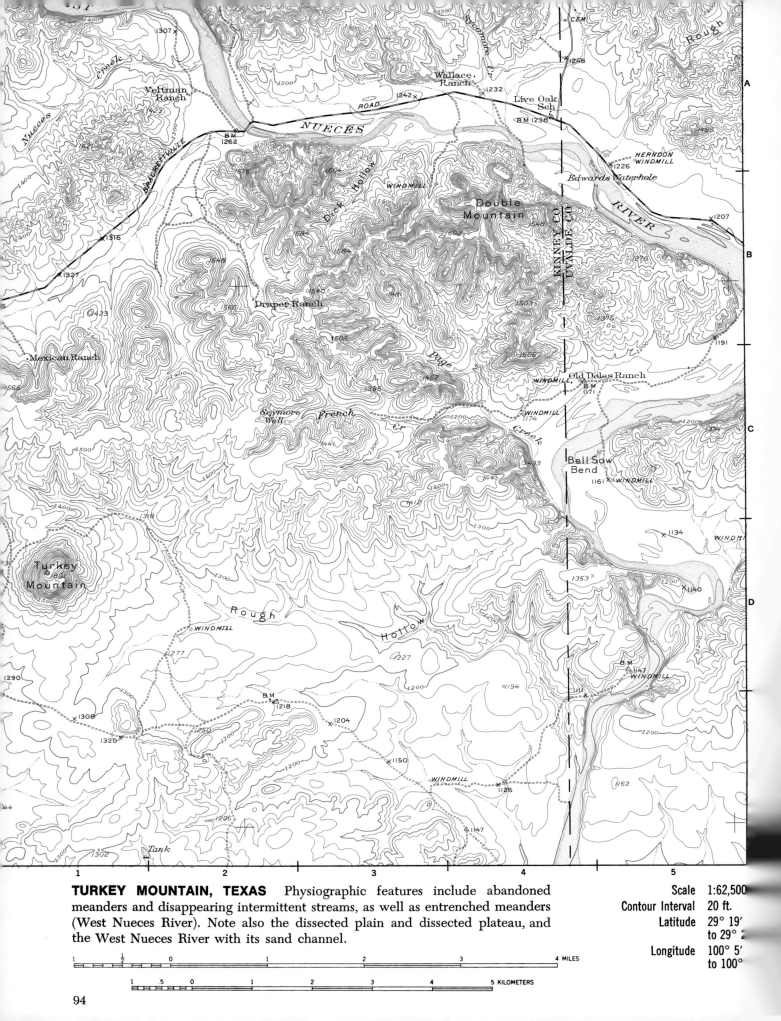

TURKEY MOUNTAIN, TEXAS Physiographic features include abandoned meanders and disappearing intermittent streams, as well as entrenched meanders (West Nueces River). Note also the dissected plain and dissected plateau, and the West Nueces River with its sand channel.

Scale 1:62,500

Contour Interval 20 ft.

Latitude 29° 19′
to 29° 2

Longitude 100° 5′
to 100°

4 MILES

5 KILOMETERS

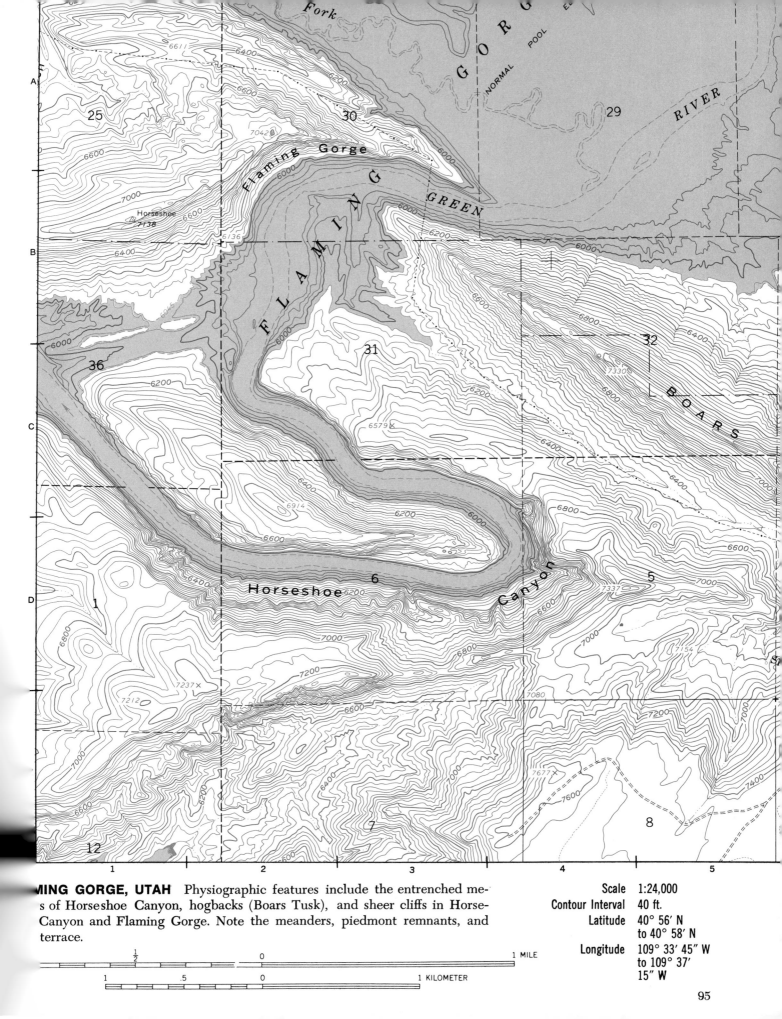

MING GORGE, UTAH Physiographic features include the entrenched me-
s of Horseshoe Canyon, hogbacks (Boars Tusk), and sheer cliffs in Horse-
Canyon and Flaming Gorge. Note the meanders, piedmont remnants, and
terrace.

Scale	1:24,000	
Contour Interval	40 ft.	
Latitude	40° 56′ N	
	to 40° 58′ N	
Longitude	109° 33′ 45″ W	
	to 109° 37′	
	15″ W	

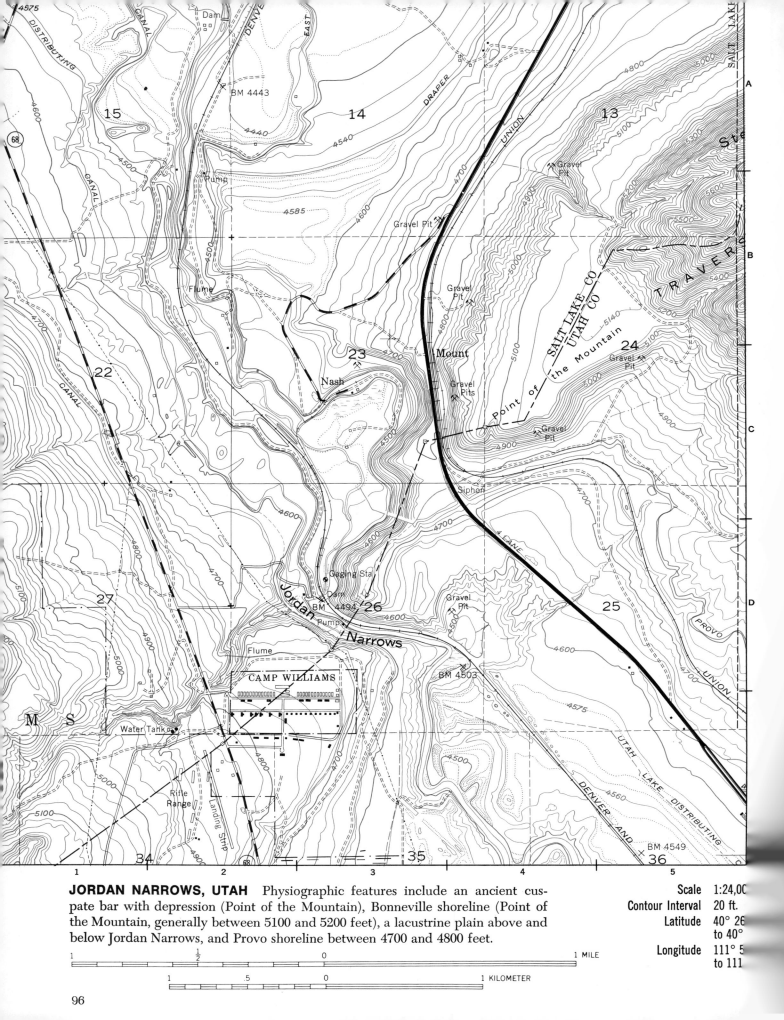

JORDAN NARROWS, UTAH Physiographic features include an ancient cuspate bar with depression (Point of the Mountain), Bonneville shoreline (Point of the Mountain, generally between 5100 and 5200 feet), a lacustrine plain above and below Jordan Narrows, and Provo shoreline between 4700 and 4800 feet.

Scale 1:24,00

Contour Interval 20 ft.

Latitude 40° 26
to 40°

Longitude 111° 5
to 111

RYSVALE, UTAH This map features a dissected plateau (portion of Sevier eau), an alluvial fan, the fault valley of the Sevier River occupying a fault desion, a flood plain, a landslide at Little Table, meanders in the Sevier River, ows.

Scale 1:62,500
Contour Interval 50 ft.
Latitude 38° 22′ N
  to 38° 29′ N
Longitude 112° 5′ W
  to 112° 14′ W

4 MILES

5 KILOMETERS

97

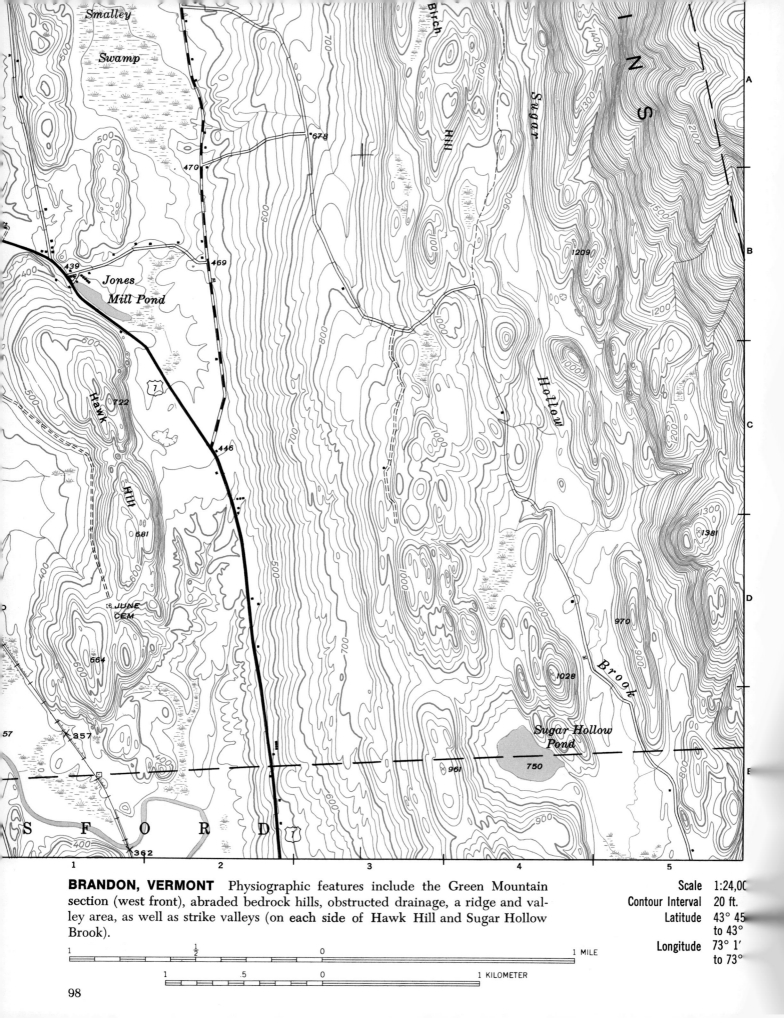

BRANDON, VERMONT Physiographic features include the Green Mountain section (west front), abraded bedrock hills, obstructed drainage, a ridge and valley area, as well as strike valleys (on each side of Hawk Hill and Sugar Hollow Brook).

Scale 1:24,00
Contour Interval 20 ft.
Latitude 43° 45
to 43°
Longitude 73° 1′
to 73°

98

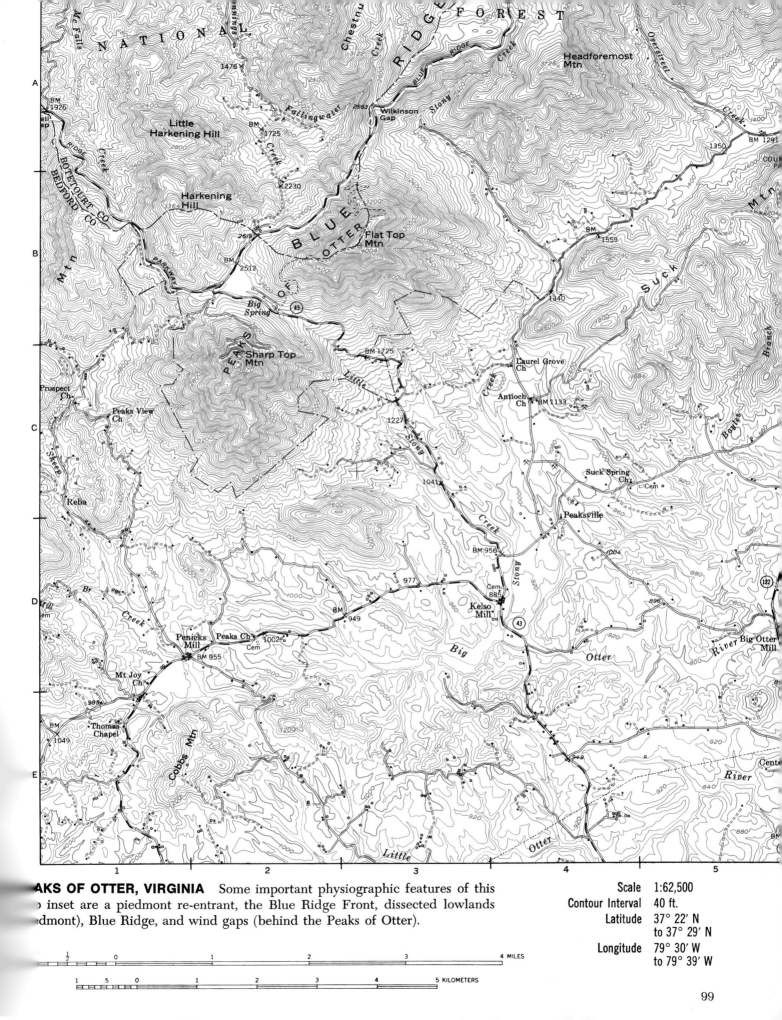

PEAKS OF OTTER, VIRGINIA   Some important physiographic features of this map inset are a piedmont re-entrant, the Blue Ridge Front, dissected lowlands (Piedmont), Blue Ridge, and wind gaps (behind the Peaks of Otter).

Scale	1:62,500
Contour Interval	40 ft.
Latitude	37° 22′ N to 37° 29′ N
Longitude	79° 30′ W to 79° 39′ W

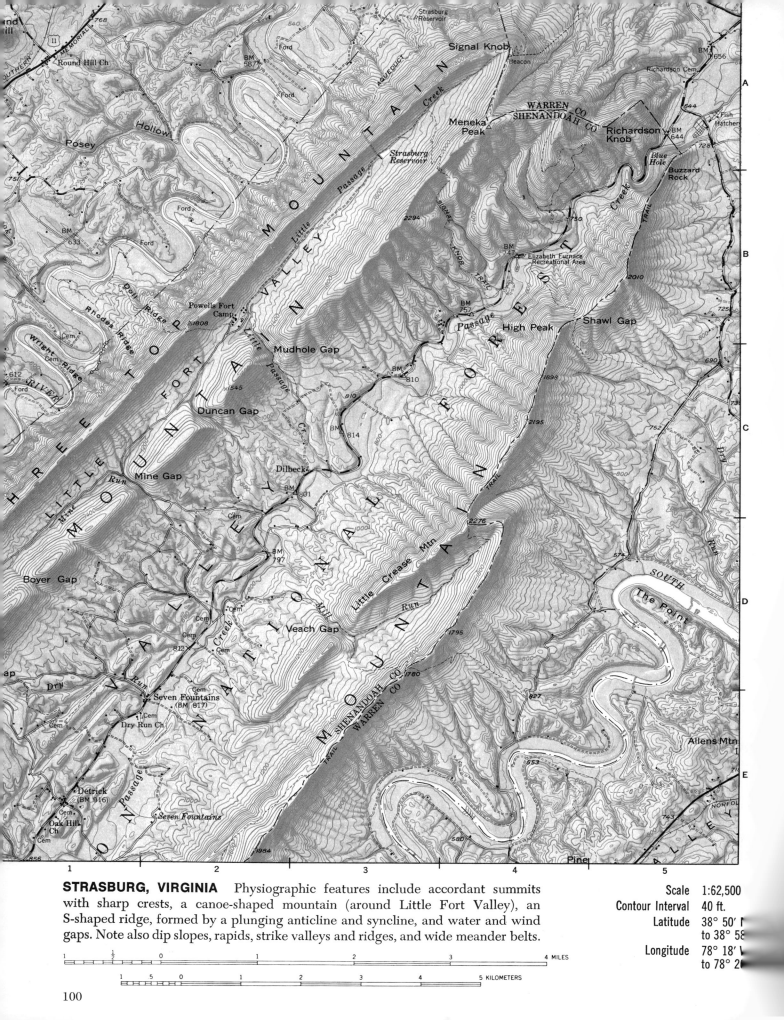

STRASBURG, VIRGINIA Physiographic features include accordant summits with sharp crests, a canoe-shaped mountain (around Little Fort Valley), an S-shaped ridge, formed by a plunging anticline and syncline, and water and wind gaps. Note also dip slopes, rapids, strike valleys and ridges, and wide meander belts.

Scale   1:62,500
Contour Interval   40 ft.
Latitude   38° 50′
to 38° 58′
Longitude   78° 18′
to 78° 2

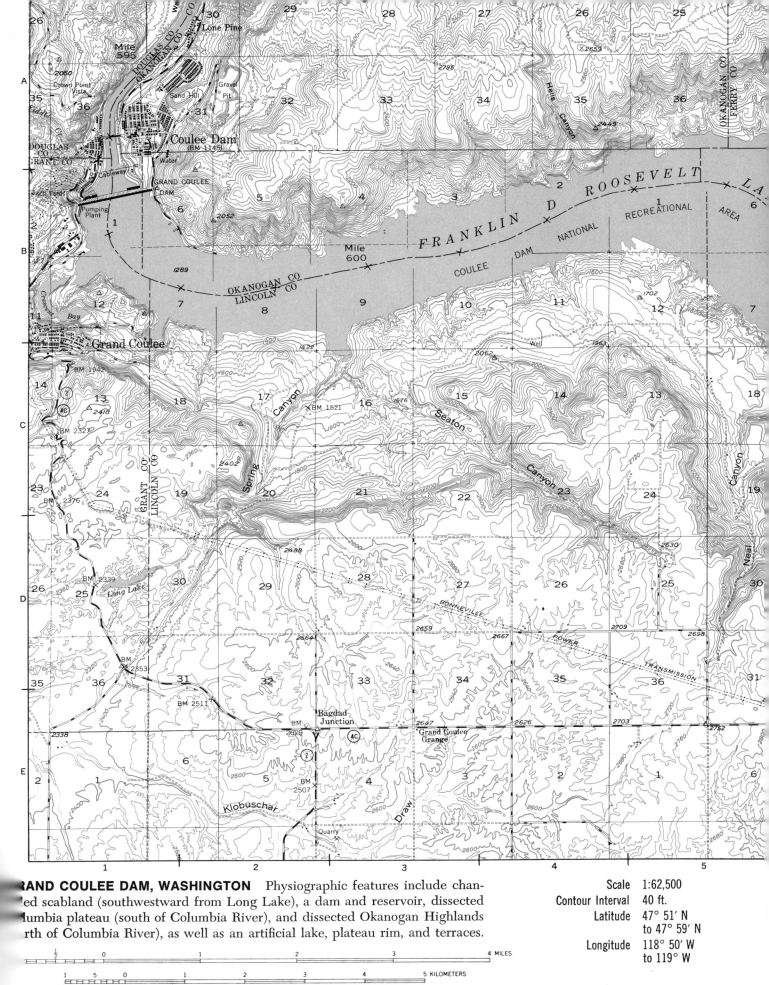

RAND COULEE DAM, WASHINGTON Physiographic features include chan-
~~~ed scabland (southwestward from Long Lake), a dam and reservoir, dissected
~~umbia plateau (south of Columbia River), and dissected Okanogan Highlands
~~rth of Columbia River), as well as an artificial lake, plateau rim, and terraces.

Scale	1:62,500
Contour Interval	40 ft.
Latitude	47° 51′ N to 47° 59′ N
Longitude	118° 50′ W to 119° W

½ 0   1   2   3   4 MILES

1 5 0   1   2   3   4   5 KILOMETERS

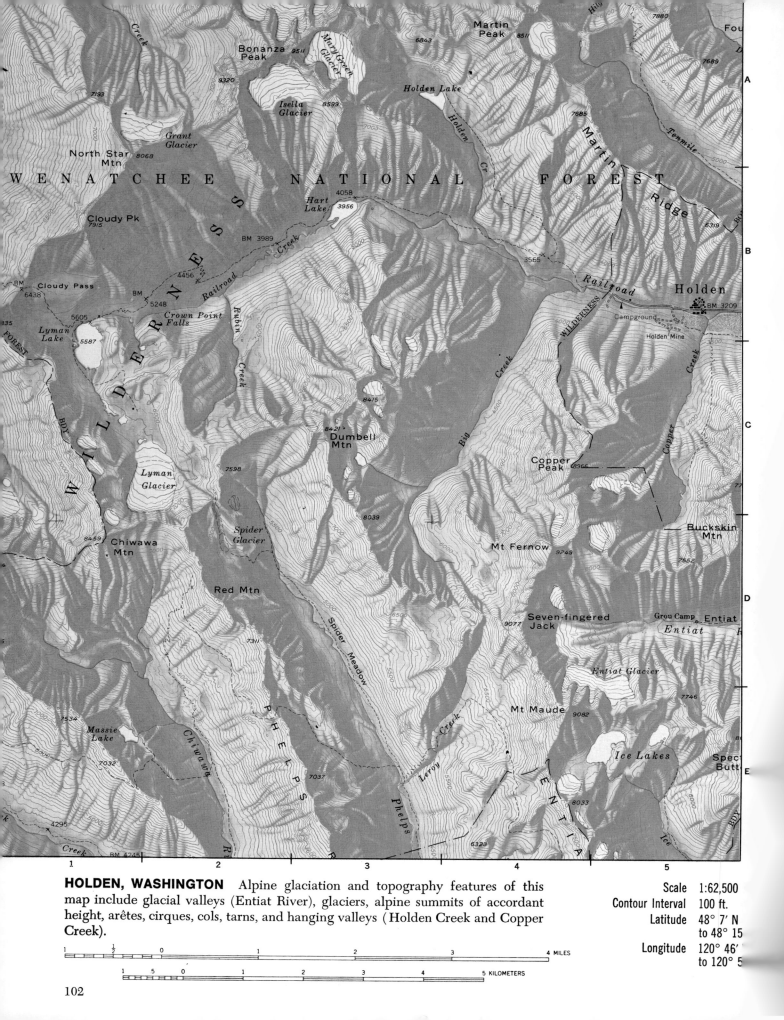

HOLDEN, WASHINGTON Alpine glaciation and topography features of this map include glacial valleys (Entiat River), glaciers, alpine summits of accordant height, arêtes, cirques, cols, tarns, and hanging valleys (Holden Creek and Copper Creek).

Scale 1:62,500
Contour Interval 100 ft.
Latitude 48° 7′ N to 48° 15
Longitude 120° 46′ to 120° 5

1   ½   0   1   2   3   4 MILES

1 5 0 1 2 3 4 5 KILOMETERS

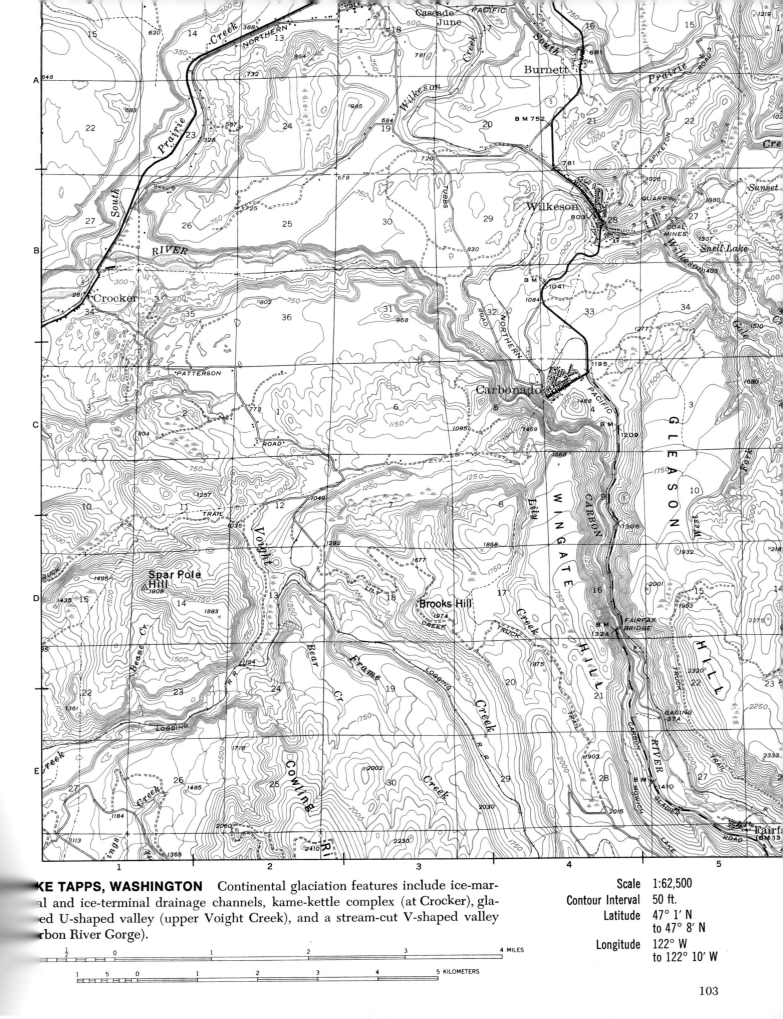

KE TAPPS, WASHINGTON Continental glaciation features include ice-mar-
al and ice-terminal drainage channels, kame-kettle complex (at Crocker), gla-
ed U-shaped valley (upper Voight Creek), and a stream-cut V-shaped valley
rbon River Gorge).

Scale	1:62,500
Contour Interval	50 ft.
Latitude	47° 1′ N
	to 47° 8′ N
Longitude	122° W
	to 122° 10′ W

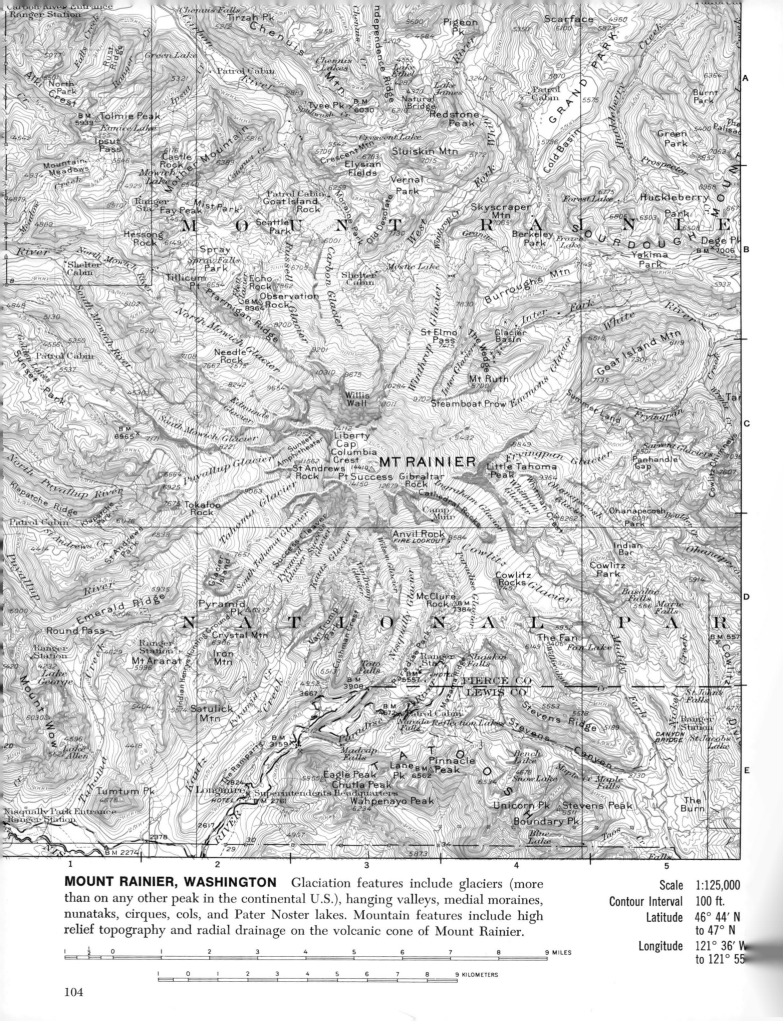

MOUNT RAINIER, WASHINGTON Glaciation features include glaciers (more than on any other peak in the continental U.S.), hanging valleys, medial moraines, nunataks, cirques, cols, and Pater Noster lakes. Mountain features include high relief topography and radial drainage on the volcanic cone of Mount Rainier.

Scale	1:125,000
Contour Interval	100 ft.
Latitude	46° 44′ N to 47° N
Longitude	121° 36′ W to 121° 55′

1 ½ 0 1 2 3 4 5 6 7 8 9 MILES

1 0 1 2 3 4 5 6 7 8 9 KILOMETERS

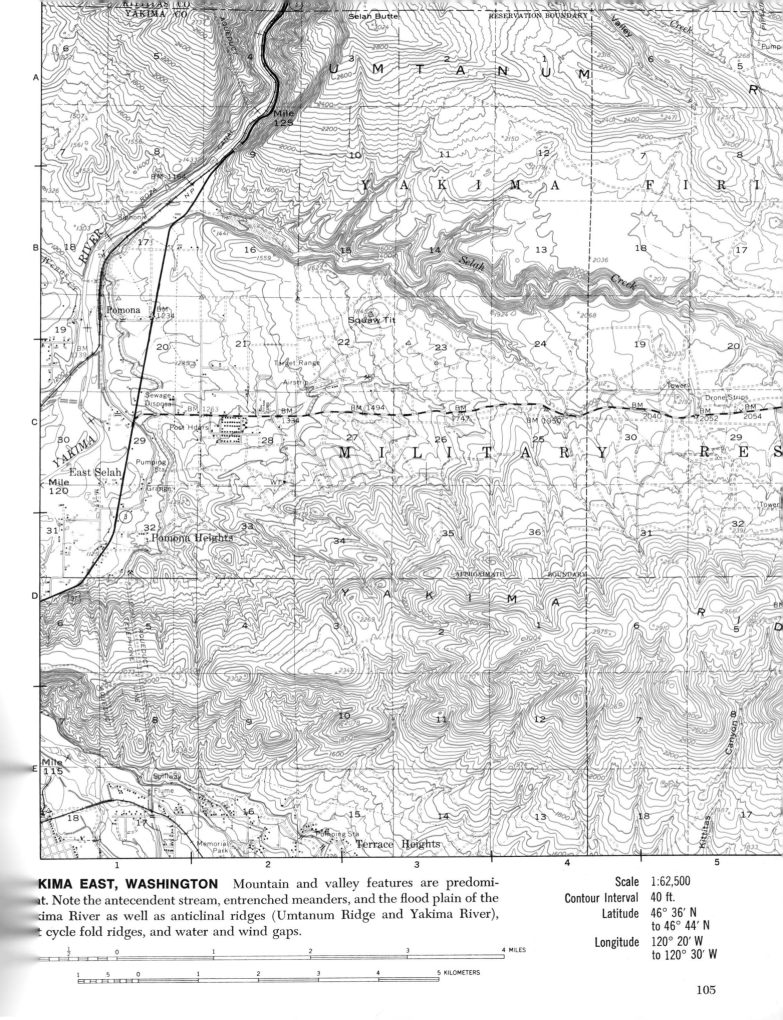

YAKIMA EAST, WASHINGTON Mountain and valley features are predomi-
...t. Note the antecedent stream, entrenched meanders, and the flood plain of the
...kima River as well as anticlinal ridges (Umtanum Ridge and Yakima River),
...t cycle fold ridges, and water and wind gaps.

Scale	1:62,500
Contour Interval	40 ft.
Latitude	46° 36′ N
	to 46° 44′ N
Longitude	120° 20′ W
	to 120° 30′ W

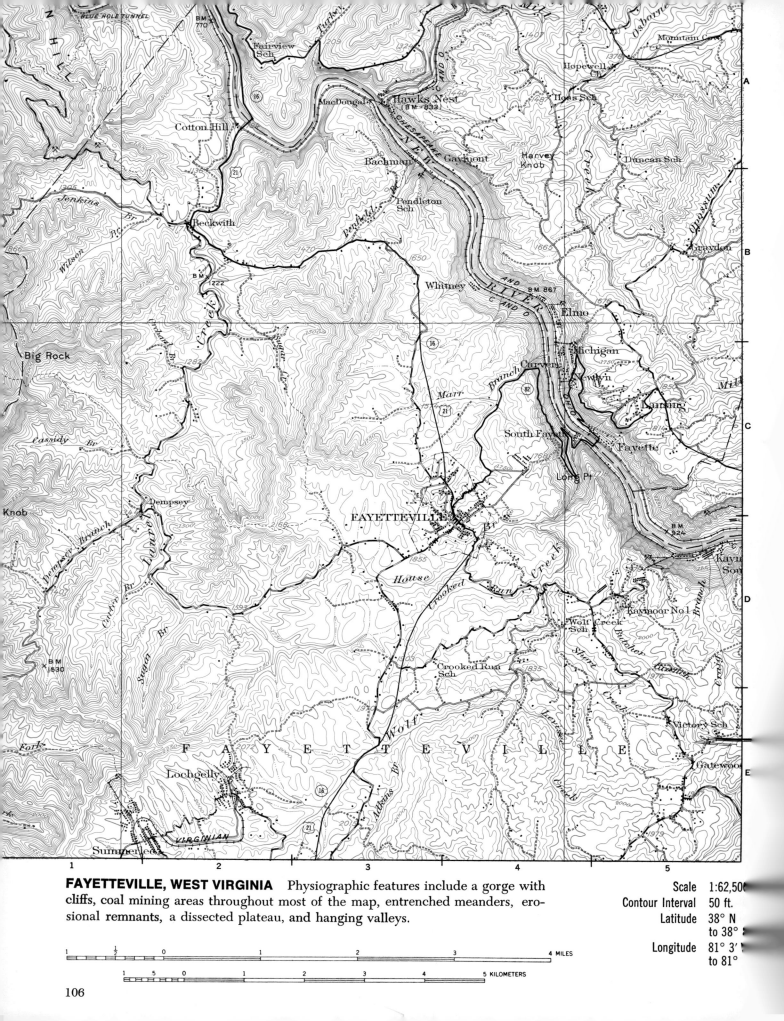

FAYETTEVILLE, WEST VIRGINIA Physiographic features include a gorge with cliffs, coal mining areas throughout most of the map, entrenched meanders, erosional remnants, a dissected plateau, and hanging valleys.

Scale   1:62,500
Contour Interval   50 ft.
Latitude   38° N
to 38°
Longitude   81° 3′
to 81°

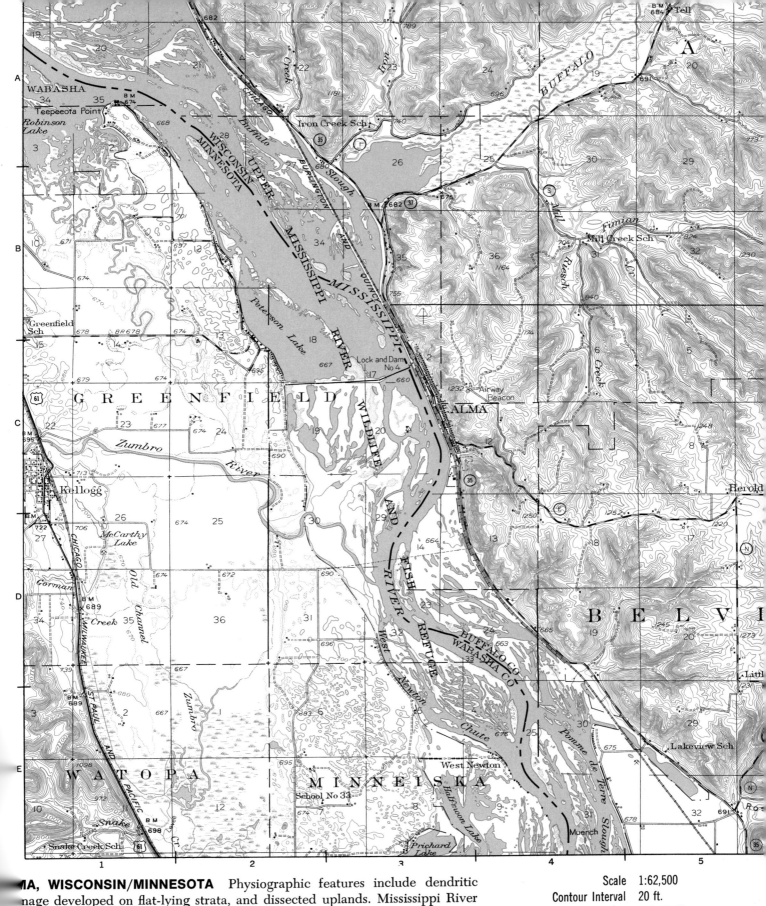

MA, WISCONSIN/MINNESOTA Physiographic features include dendritic
drainage developed on flat-lying strata, and dissected uplands. Mississippi River
features also include flood control and navigation development, a flood plain, and
bars.

Scale	1:62,500
Contour Interval	20 ft.
Latitude	44° 15′ N
	to 44° 23′ N
Longitude	91° 51′ W
	to 92° W

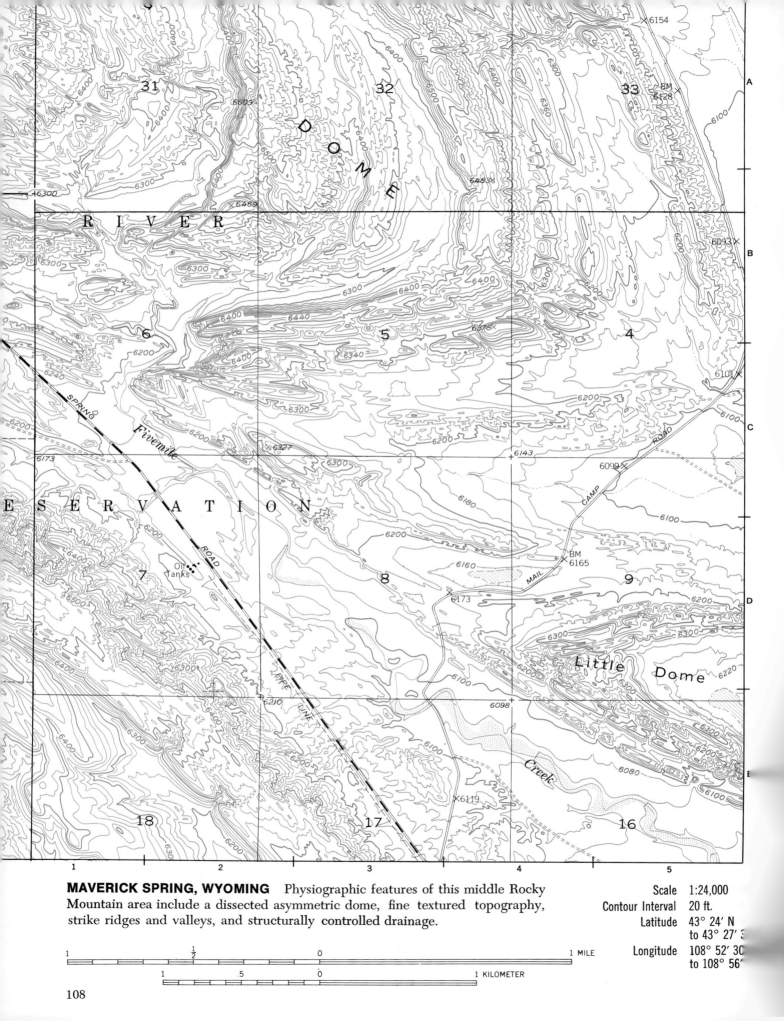

MAVERICK SPRING, WYOMING Physiographic features of this middle Rocky Mountain area include a dissected asymmetric dome, fine textured topography, strike ridges and valleys, and structurally controlled drainage.

Scale 1:24,000
Contour Interval 20 ft.
Latitude 43° 24′ N
to 43° 27′ 3
Longitude 108° 52′ 30
to 108° 56′

1 MILE

1 KILOMETER

108

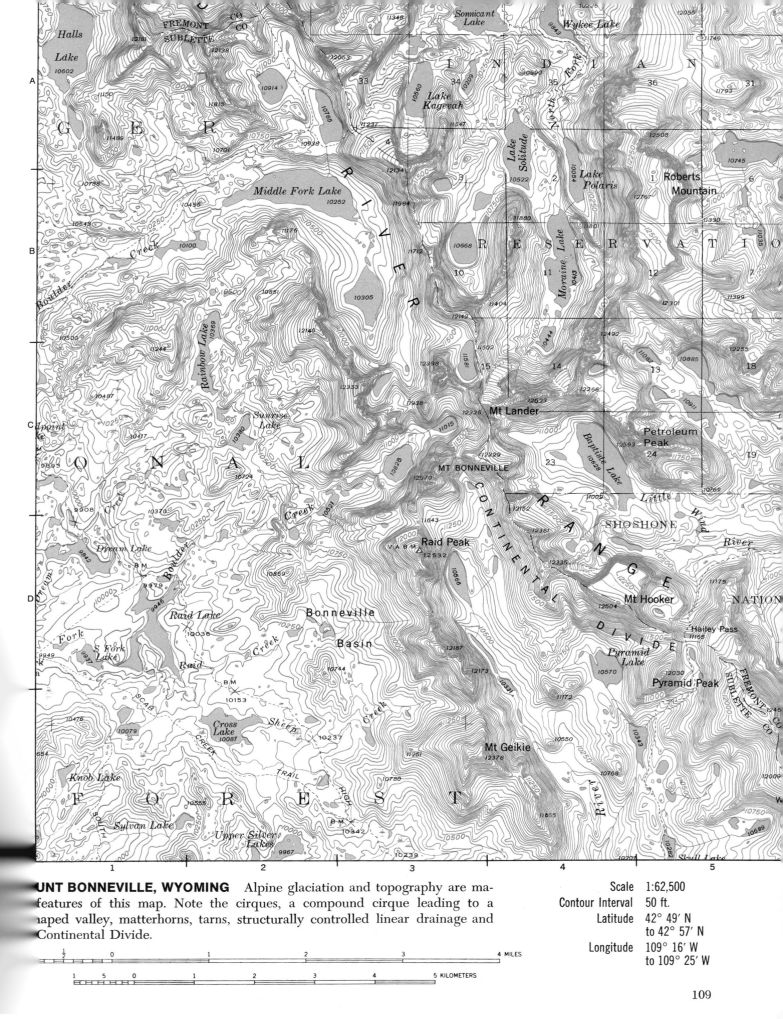

UNT BONNEVILLE, WYOMING   Alpine glaciation and topography are ma-features of this map. Note the cirques, a compound cirque leading to a naped valley, matterhorns, tarns, structurally controlled linear drainage and Continental Divide.

Scale   1:62,500

Contour Interval   50 ft.

Latitude   42° 49′ N
to 42° 57′ N

Longitude   109° 16′ W
to 109° 25′ W

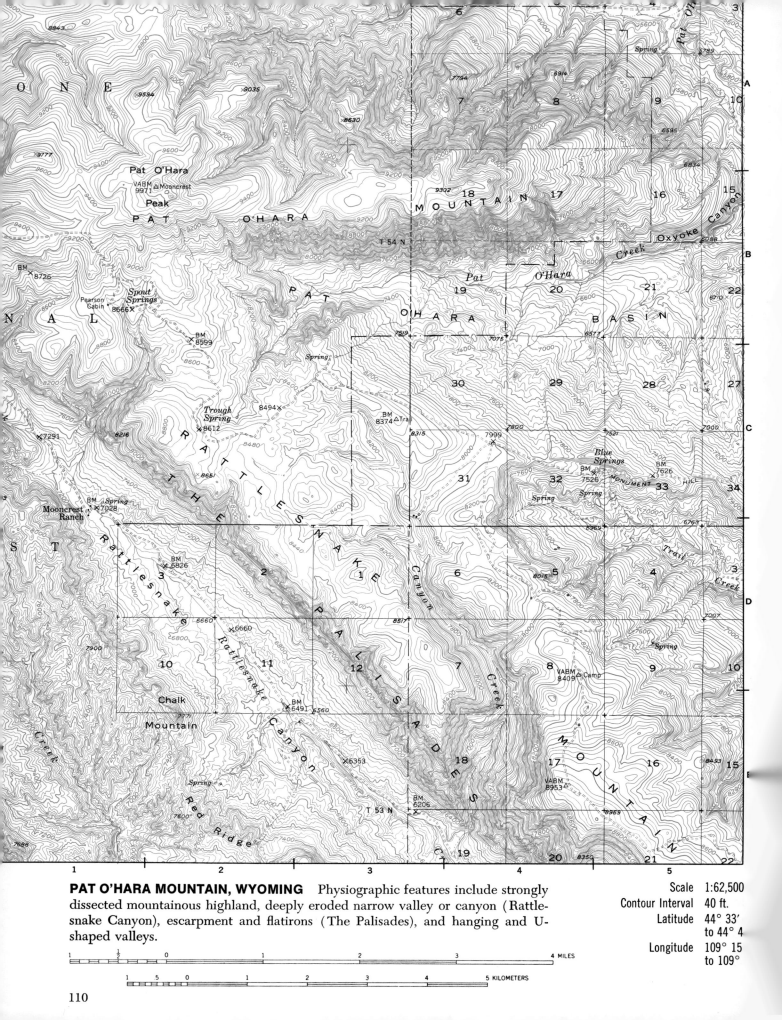

PAT O'HARA MOUNTAIN, WYOMING   Physiographic features include strongly dissected mountainous highland, deeply eroded narrow valley or canyon (Rattlesnake Canyon), escarpment and flatirons (The Palisades), and hanging and U-shaped valleys.

Scale   1:62,500
Contour Interval   40 ft.
Latitude   44° 33′
to 44° 4
Longitude   109° 15
to 109°

Appendix: United States Physical Divisions

MAJOR DIVISION	PROVINCE	SECTION	CHARACTERISTICS
Laurentian Upland	1. Superior Upland		1. Submaturely dissected, recently glaciated peneplain on crystalline rocks of complex structure.
Atlantic Plain	2. Continental Shelf		2. Sloping submarine plain of sedimentation.
	3. Coastal Plain	a. Embayed section	3a. Submaturely dissected and partly submerged, terraced coastal plain.
		b. Sea Island section	3b. Young to mature terraced coastal plain with submerged border.
		c. Floridian section	3c. Young marine plain, with sand hills, swamps, sinks, and lakes.
		d. East Gulf Coastal Plain	3d. Young to mature belted coastal plain.
		e. Mississippi Alluvial Plain	3e. Flood plain and delta.
		f. West Gulf Coastal Plain	3f. Young grading inland to mature coastal plain.
Appalachian Highlands	4. Piedmont province	a. Piedmont Upland	4a. Submaturely dissected peneplain on disordered resistant rocks; moderate relief.
		b. Piedmont Lowlands	4b. Less uplifted peneplain on weak strata, residual ridges on strong rocks.
	5. Blue Ridge province	a. Northern section	5a. Maturely dissected mountains of crystalline rocks; accordant altitudes.
		b. Southern section	5b. Suddued mountains of disordered crystalline rocks.
	6. Valley and Ridge province	a. Tennessee section	6a. 2nd-cycle mountains of folded strong and weak strata; valley belts predominate over even-crested ridges.
		b. Middle section	6b. The same, but even-crested ridges predominate over valleys except on east side.
		c. Hudson Valley	6c. Glaciated peneplain on weak folded strata.
	7. St. Lawrence Valley	a. Champlain section	7a. Rolling lowland, glaciated; in part covered by young marine plain.
		b. Northern section	7b. Young marine plain with local rock hills.
	8. Appalachian Plateaus	a. Mohawk section	8a. Maturely dissected glaciated plateau; varied relief and diverse altitudes.
		b. Catskill section	8b. Maturely dissected plateau of mountainous relief and coarse texture (glaciated).
		c. Southern New York section	8c. Mature glaciated plateau of moderate relief.
		d. Allegheny Mountain section	8d. Mature plateau of strong relief; some mountains due to erosion of open folds.
		e. Kanawha section	8e. Mature plateau of fine texture; moderate to strong relief.
		f. Cumberland Plateau section	8f. Submaturely dissected plateau of moderate to strong relief.
		g. Cumberland Mountain section	8g. Higher mature plateau and mountain ridges on eroded open folds.
	9. New England province	a. Seaboard Lowland section	9a. Peneplains below 500 feet postmaturely eroded and glaciated; few monadnocks.
		b. New England Upland section	9b. Dissected and glaciated peneplains on complex structural features; monadnocks.
		c. White Mountain section	9c. Subdued glaciated mountain masses of crystalline rocks.
		d. Green Mountain section	9d. Linear ranges of subdued and glaciated mountains and residual plateaus.
		e. Taconic section	9e. Maturely dissected and glaciated mountains and peneplain on resistant folded strata.
	10. Adirondack province		10. Subdued mountains and dissected peneplain, glaciated.

MAJOR DIVISION	PROVINCE	SECTION	CHARACTERISTICS
Interior Plains	11. Interior Low Plateaus	a. Highland Rim section ...... 11a.	Young to mature plateau of moderate relief.
		b. Lexington Plain .... 11b.	Mature to old plain on weak rocks; trenched by main rivers.
		c. Nashville Basin .... 11c.	Mature to old plain on weak rocks; slightly uplifted and moderately dissected.
		d. Possible western section (not delimited)......... 11d.	Low, maturely dissected plateau with silt-filled valleys.
	12. Central Lowland	a. Eastern lake section .... 12a.	Maturely dissected and glaciated cuestas and low-lands; moraines, lakes, and lacustrine plains.
		b. Western lake section .... 12b.	Young glaciated plain; moraines, lakes, and lacustrine plains.
		c. Wisconsin Driftless section .. 12c.	Maturely dissected plateau and lowland invaded by glacial outwash. (Margin of old eroded drift incl.)
		d. Till Plains .... 12d.	Young till plains; morainic topography rare; no lakes.
		e. Dissected Till Plains .... 12e.	Submaturely to maturely dissected till plains.
		f. Osage Plains .... 12f.	Old scarped plains beveling faintly inclined strata; main streams intrenched.
	13. Great Plains province	a. Missouri Plateau, glaciated .. 13a.	Glaciated old plateaus; isolated mountains.
		b. Missouri Plateau, unglaciated 13b.	Old plateau; terrace lands; local badlands; isolated mountains.
		c. Black Hills .... 13c.	Maturely dissected domed mountains.
		d. High Plains .... 13d.	Broad intervalley remnants of smooth fluviatile plains.
		e. Plains Border .... 13e.	Submaturely to maturely dissected plateau.
		f. Colorado Piedmont .... 13f.	Late mature to old elevated plain.
		g. Raton section .... 13g.	Trenched peneplain surmounted by dissected, lava capped plateaus and buttes.
		h. Pecos Valley .... 13h.	Late mature to old plain.
		i. Edwards Plateau .... 13i.	Young plateau with mature margin of moderate t strong relief.
		k. Central Texas section ...... 13k.	Plateau in maturity and later stages of erosion.
Interior Highlands	14. Ozark Plateaus	a. Springfield-Salem plateaus .. 14a.	Submature to mature plateaus.
		b. Boston "Mountains" .... 14b.	Submature to mature plateau of strong relief.
	15. Ouachita province	a. Arkansas Valley .... 15a.	Gently folded strong and weak strata; peneplain wi residual ridges.
		b. Ouachita Mountains .... 15b.	Second-cycle mountains of folded strong and we strata.
Rocky Mountain System	16. Southern Rocky Mountains	.... 16.	Complex mountains of various types; intermo basins.
	17. Wyoming Basin	.... 17.	Elevated plains in various stages of erosion; isolat low mountains.
	18. Middle Rocky Mountains	.... 18.	Complex mountains, mainly anticlinal ranges; int mont basins.
	19. Northern Rocky Mountains	.... 19.	Deeply dissected mountain uplands, not anticli ranges; intermont basins.

MAJOR DIVISION	PROVINCE	SECTION	CHARACTERISTICS
Intermontane Plateaus	20. Columbia Plateaus	a. Walla Walla Plateau .... 20a.	Rolling plateau with young incised valleys.
		b. Blue Mountain section ...... 20b.	Complex mountains and dissected volcanic plateaus.
		c. Payette section .... 20c.	Young plateaus of prevailingly weak rocks; broad alluvial terraces. (Applies to northern part only.)
		d. Snake River Plain .... 20d.	Young lava plateau.
		e. Harney section .... 20e.	Young lava plateau; features of recent volcanism; ineffective drainage.
	21. Colorado Plateaus	a. High Plateaus of Utah ...... 21a.	High block plateaus, in part lava-capped; terraced plateaus on south side.
		b. Uinta Basin .... 21b.	Dissected plateau; strong relief.
		c. Canyon Lands .... 21c.	Young to mature canyoned plateaus; high relief.
		d. Navajo section .... 21d.	Young plateaus; smaller relief than 21c, into which it grades.
		e. Grand Canyon section ..... 21e.	High block plateaus, trenched by Grand Canyon.
		f. Datil section .... 21f.	Lava flows entire or in remnants; volcanic necks.
	22. Basin and Range province	a. Great Basin .... 22a.	Isolated ranges (largely dissected block mountains) separated by aggraded desert plains.
		b. Sonoran Desert .... 22b.	Widely separated short ranges in desert plains.
		c. Salton Trough .... 22c.	Desert alluvial slopes and delta plain; Gulf of California.
		d. Mexican Highland .... 22d.	Isolated ranges (largely dissected block mountains) separated by aggraded desert plains.
		e. Sacramento section .... 22e.	Mature block mountains of gently tilted strata; block plateaus; bolsons.
Pacific Mountain System	23. Cascade-Sierra Mountains	a. Northern Cascade Mountains. 23a.	Sharp alpine summits of accordant height; higher volcanic cones.
		b. Middle Cascade Mountains .. 23b.	Generally accordant summits; higher volcanic cones.
		c. Southern Cascade Mountains. 23c.	Volcanic mountains variously eroded; no very distinct range.
		d. Sierra Nevada .... 23d.	Block mountain range tilted west; accordant crests; alpine peaks near east side.
	24. Pacific Border province	a. Puget Trough .... 24a.	Lowlands of diverse character; in part submerged.
		b. Olympic Mountains .... 24b.	Generally accordant crests; local alpine peaks.
		c. Oregon Coast Range .... 24c.	Uplifted peneplain on weak rocks; dissected; monadnocks of igneous rock.
		d. Klamath Mountains .... 24d.	Uplifted and dissected peneplain on strong rocks; extensive monadnock ranges.
		e. California Trough .... 24e.	Low fluviatile plain.
		f. California Coast Ranges .... 24f.	Parallel ranges and valleys on folded, faulted, and metamorphosed strata; rounded crests of subequal height.
	25. Lower Californian province	g. Los Angeles Ranges .... 24g.	Narrow ranges and broad fault blocks; alluviated lowlands.
		.... 25.	Dissected westward-sloping granite upland (in northern part).

Appendix: United States Physical Divisions

24b
23a
LAKE TAPPS
HOLDEN
GRAND COULEE DAM
CHIEF MOUNTAIN
24A
MOUNT RAINIER
YAKIMA EAST
20a
24c
19
13a
LANSFO
VOLT
PELICAN LAKE
BANDON
23b
20e
13b
GALICE
CHEMULT
ENNIS
CRATER LAKE
NATIONAL PARK
AND VICINITY
MENAN BUTTES
PAT O'HARA MOUNTAIN
18
MAVERICK SPRING
13c
20b
24d
BRAY
20c
20d
HOT SPRINGS
23c
THOUSAND SPRINGS
MOUNT BONNEVILLE
SHEEP MOUNT
SONOMA RANGE
17
ASHBY
JORDAN NARROWS
FLAMING GORGE
13d
POINT REYES
23d
22a
ANVIL POINTS
21b
COMMERCE CITY
24f
24e
HOLY CROSS
13f
MOUNT TOM
MARYSVALE
21a
21c
JUANITA ARCH
16
CO
FURNACE CREEK
LAKE
SHIP ROCK
13g
VENTURA
BRIGHT ANGEL
21d
24g
21e
13d
SAN LUIS REY
PROMONTORY BUTTE
21f
22b
13h
22c
ANTELOPE PEAK
22d
BOTTOMLESS LAKES
22e
GUADALUPE PEAK
13i
SANTIAGO PEAK

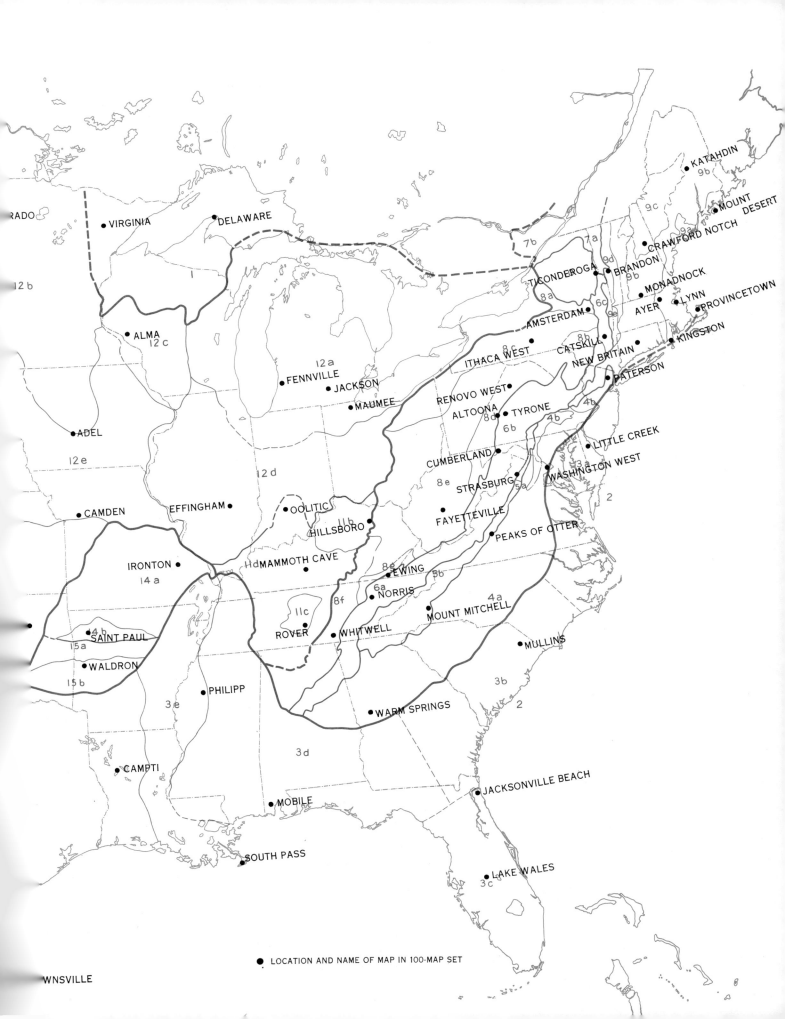

RADO

VIRGINIA

DELAWARE

KATAHDIN
9b

MOUNT DESERT

9c

CRAWFORD NOTCH

7b   7a

12 b

9d   BRANDON
TICONDEROGA   9b

MONADNOCK

ALMA
12 c

8a
6c   AYER   LYNN
PROVINCETOWN
AMSTERDAM   9e

12 a

ITHACA WEST   8c   CATSKILL
NEW BRITAIN   8b   KINGSTON

FENNVILLE   PATERSON

JACKSON

RENOVO WEST

MAUMEE   ALTOONA 8d   TYRONE   4b
8d   6b   4b

ADEL   CUMBERLAND   LITTLE CREEK

12 e   8e   WASHINGTON WEST
STRASBURG   5a
6b

CAMDEN   EFFINGHAM   OOLITIC   12 d   FAYETTEVILLE   2

HILLSBORO   11b   PEAKS OF OTTER

IRONTON   Hd MAMMOTH CAVE   8e   5b
14 a   EWING
6a   NORRIS

4b   11c   8f   MOUNT MITCHELL   4a
SAINT PAUL
15 a   ROVER   WHITWELL

WALDRON   MULLINS

15 b

PHILIPP   3e   3b

WARM SPRINGS   2

3 d

CAMPTI

JACKSONVILLE BEACH

MOBILE

SOUTH PASS

LAKE WALES
3c

● LOCATION AND NAME OF MAP IN 100-MAP SET

WNSVILLE

Index to physiographic features by map

In this index, the major physiographic features for each map are listed alphabetically under the title of the map. The index is arranged alphabetically by states, the same order that is followed in the text of the book. To locate specific features when the map is not known or to compare an individual feature that appears on more than one map, see the comprehensive listing in the *Index to Physiographic Features by Feature*, beginning on p. 124

ALABAMA

Mobile, 11

East Gulf Coastal Plain

Abandoned Pleistocene shoreline
(Pamlico shoreline, foot of bluffs, about 30-foot level, through center of map)
Dissected plain
Drowned valleys (on marine terrace)
Marine terrace (Pamlico terrace, swampy, adjacent to Mobile Bay and below the 30-foot level)
Partially obstructed outlet (Dog River)
Tidal marsh or swamp

ARIZONA

Antelope Peak, 12

Sonoran Desert

Alluvial fan
Arroyo
Bajada
Desert plain
Erosional remnant (Antelope Peak)
Island mountains (inselbergs)
Parallel drainage on pediment
Pediment
Short mountain range
Wash

Bright Angel, 13

Grand Canyon Section

Butte (Dana Butte, Summer Butte, etc.)
Cliffs (banded contouring)
Dissected plateau of strong relief
Encroachment of younger upon older drainage (south portion of map)
Fault line valley (Bright Angel Canyon)
Gorge (Granite Gorge)
Grand Canyon of the Colorado River
Migrating divide (south portion of map)
Plateaus (Coconino)
Points (Grandeur, Hopi, etc.)
Rapids (Granite Rapids, etc.)
Rock terrace
Tonto Platform (lower rim of canyon, at Plateau Point, etc.)
V-shaped valley

Promontory Butte, 14

Mexican Highland (and Grand Canyon Section)

Canyon or gorge (Tonto Creek)
Dissected highland (south of Mogollon Rim)
Escarpment (Mogollon Rim)
Mesa (Mogollon Mesa, north portion of map)
Parallel consequent drainage (on Mogollon Mesa)

ARKANSAS

Saint Paul, 15

Ozark Plateaus—Boston Mountains
Dendritic drainage (Delaney Creek, etc.)
Dissected plateau
Flood plain
Remnants of plateau surface (Brannon Mountain, etc.)
River bluff and terrace
Undercut slope

Waldron, 16

Ouachita Mountains
Folded mountains (2nd cycle, strong and weak rocks)
Folds en echelon
Hogbacks
Knob
Ridges (formed of folded hard strata)
Strike ridges and valleys
Structurally controlled drainage (trellis type north portion of map)
Trellis drainage
Water gap (Poteau River, etc.)

CALIFORNIA

Bray, 17

Southern Cascade Mountains
Butte
Cinder cones
Collapse depressions (in Red Rock Valley)
Disappearing intermittent streams
Eroded volcanic mountains
Ice cave

Furnace Creek, 18

Basin and Range Province
Great Basin Section
Alluvial fans, coalescing (or bajada)
Alluvial fan, dissected
Bolson (Death Valley)
Dissected block mountains
Dissected foothills (fan shaped)
Fault-line scarp (west face of Black Mountains)
Island mountains (inselbergs)
Mineral springs (Travertine Springs)
Mining areas (Gower Gulch)
Playa
Sea level and below sea level contours to minus 280

Mount Tom, 19

Sierra Nevada (also portion of Great Basin)
Alluvial fan, dissected
Alpine topography
Arête
Basin
Cirque
Cirque headwall
Cirque lake
Col
Cyclopean stairs
Eastern escarpment of Sierra Nevada (through west central portion of map)
Glacial trough
Glaciers
Hanging valley
Lateral moraine
Pass
Pater Noster lakes
Tarns
U-shaped valleys (Pine Creek)

Point Reyes, 20

Pacific Border Province
California Coast Range
Barrier beach (offset) (at Drakes Bay)
Battered sea cliff (Point Reyes and Drakes Head)
Baymouth bar
Block mountain (Inverness Ridge)
Cape (Point Reyes)
Drainage (blocked by barrier beach)
Estuary (Drakes Estero)
Headland, truncated (Point Reyes, etc.)
Lagoons or coastal lakes (see estuary)
Marine terrace
Parallel ranges and valleys
Sand dunes
Sand spit
Sea stacks
Tidal flat (at Point Reyes Station)
Wave-cut cliff

San Luis Rey, 21

Lower California Province
Barrier beaches
Lagoon
Marine terraces

Terraced lowland (west portion of map
adjacent to Gulf of Santa Catalina)

Ventura, 22

Pacific Border Province
Los Angeles Ranges
Alluvial fan
Alluviated lowland
Beach
Coastal plain
Delta (Ventura River)
Dissected upland
Landslide area
Marine terraces
Obstructed drainage
(mouth of Ventura River)
River in flood plain with sand channel
Underwater contours (depth curves)

COLORADO

Anvil Points, 23

Colorado Plateaus—Uinta Basin Section
Dissected plateau of strong relief
Escarpment
Oil shale mines

Commerce City, 24

Great Plains
Colorado Piedmont Section
Canals (irrigation system)
Deflation depressions
Dissected pediment
(northwest portion of map)
Flood plain (South Platte River)
River bluffs
Sand pits (industrial)
Terrace, east side of South Platte
River, known as Broadway Terrace
and well defined

Holy Cross, 25

Southern Rocky Mountains
Alpine topography
Cirque (Isolation Lake, Lonesome
Lake, etc.)
Cirque lake
Continental Divide
Contrasting topography between
mountains of Pre-Cambrian rocks,
west portion of map, and mountains
of sedimentary rocks, east portion
of map
Cyclopean stairs
Glacial valley
Hanging valley
(Mill Creek and Glacier Creek)
Intermont basin
Mineralized area, gold, lead, silver,
zinc
Tarn (Deckers Lake, etc.)
Terminal moraines (at Sylvan Lake
and Turquoise Lake)

Juanita Arch, 26

Colorado Plateaus
Canyon Lands
Canyon, V-shaped

Canyon or gorge (Dolores River)
Cliffs
Dry Falls
Escarpments at rim of Dolores River
Esplanade
High relief topography
Mesa
Natural bridge (Juanita Arch)

CONNECTICUT

New Britain, 27

New England Uplands
Alluvial plain
(northwest portion of map)
Drainage reversal, glacial (Pequabuck
River flowing north where
Farmington River formerly flowed
south)
Fault block mountains
Kettles (northwest portion)
Lava with irregular surface
(Bradley Mountain)
Outwash terraces
(west portion of map)
Stream piracy, pre-glacial
(at Plainville)
Wind gap—ancient water gap of
ancestral Connecticut
River (Cooks Gap)
Swamps (Dead Wood Swamp, etc.)

DELAWARE

Little Creek, 28

Coastal Plain
Embayed Section
Artificial drainage ditches (parallel)
Coastal terrace (Pamlico terrace),
weakly dissected and above the 6
to 8 foot level
Silver Bluff terrace (swampy),
below 6 to 8 foot level
Silver Bluff shoreline
Tidal meanders
Tidal swamp (bordering the bay)

DISTRICT OF COLUMBIA/VIRGINIA

Washington West, 29

Coastal Plain and Piedmont Upland
Channel (small ships)
Dissected depositional surface
(Coastal Plain)
Dissected erosional surface
(Piedmont)
Drowned river (Potomac River
below Key Bridge)
Entrenched stream (Potomac River
above Key Bridge)
Fall line (dividing line between
Piedmont and Coastal Plain, along
Florida Avenue, etc.)

FLORIDA

Jacksonville Beach, 30

Coastal Plain
Floridian Section
Ancient beach ridges
Barrier beaches, 3 series
Beaches, along Atlantic Ocean
Dunes and beach ridges
Prograded shore
Silver Bluff shoreline, post-Pleistocene
(at elevation of 6 to 8 feet)
Swamp
Tidal swamp

Lake Wales, 31

Coastal Plain—Floridian Section
Artificial drainage canal
Deep lakes and deep dry depressions
(sinks formed by solution of sub-
surface limestone)
Poorly defined surface drainage

GEORGIA

Warm Springs, 32

Piedmont Upland
Basin (eroded in soft rocks in a
structural dome—The Cove)
Dissected peneplain surface
Gorge
Resistant rock ridges (steeply dipping
and folded—Pine Mountain and
Oak Mountain)
Superposed stream (Flint River)
Warm Springs (Mineral Springs)
Water gap
Wind gap

IDAHO

Menan Buttes, 33

*Note: See Thousand Springs (Idaho)
for older, related features.*
Snake River Plain
Check dams
Cinder cones (Menan Buttes)
Craters (Menan Buttes)
Depression contours (northwest
portion of map and in craters of
Menan Buttes)
Flood plain
Irrigation system with canals
Meander scars (along Henrys Fork)
Meandering streams in flood plain

Thousand Springs, 34

*Note: See Menan Buttes (Idaho) for
related features.*
Snake River Plain
Abandoned channel
Canyon
Erosional remnant
Escarpments (at rim of canyon, etc.)
Hot springs
Hot water wells

117

IDAHO

Thousand Springs, 34 *(continued)*

Plain (former wide valley filled with lava flows, northeast portion of map)
Rapids (due to hard and soft layers)
Springs at various levels, right bank Snake River, fed from underground streams following buried river channels and intercepted by north flowing tangent of Snake River

ILLINOIS

Effingham, 35

Central Lowland—Till Plains
End moraine (position controlled by bedrock ridge) running northeast-southwest through Shumway
Dendritic drainage
Dissected till plain, with loess mantle (Illinoian Age)
Gullied stream channels in flood plains
Integrated drainage on end moraine

INDIANA

Oolitic, 36

Interior Low Plateaus
Abandoned meander (at Crooked Creek)
Dissected plateau (west half of map)
Entrenched meanders (White River)
Karst topography (east portion of map)
Limestone quarries
Meander core at Crooked Creek
Meander spurs (Horseshoe Bend)
Sinks (limestone)
Slip-off slope (along White River)
Undercut slopes (along White River)

IOWA

Adel, 37

Central Lowland
Dissected Till Plains and Western Lake Section
Cutoff meander
Dendritic drainage
Dissected till plains (south and east portions of map)
Flood plain, narrow
Former river channel (along C. M. St. P. & P. RR.)
Glaciated plain, mantled with loess (north portion of map)
Slough
Stream capture (lower Panther Creek)

KANSAS

Lake McBride, 38

Great Plains Province
Plains Border and High Plains Sections
Artificial lake
Bluffs
Dissected high plain
Gullied stream channel

KENTUCKY/VIRGINIA

Ewing, 39

Appalachian Plateaus
Cumberland Mountain Section (also Valley and Ridge Province)
Cumberland Front (across center of the map)
Escarpment (Cumberland Mountain)
Hogback (Poor Valley Ridge)
Ridge (Poor Ridge)
Sink holes
Strike valley (Poor Valley)
Strongly dissected plateau
Structurally controlled drainage (south portion of map)
Water gaps

KENTUCKY

Hillsboro, 40

Interior Low Plateaus
Lexington Plain (also portion of Appalachian Plateaus)
Dendritic drainage, rectangular, joint-controlled (Turkey Run, etc.)
Entrenched stream (Licking River)
Former meander channel now occupied by Indian Creek
Imminent stream piracy at bend in Buttermilk Branch
Outliers of Appalachian Plateau
Ridges of accordant height (east side of map)
River bluff
River terraces (Licking River)
Slip-off slopes (on Licking River)
Stock watering pond
Stream capture (Turkey Run)
Terraced floodplain
Undercut slopes (on Licking River)

Mammoth Cave, 41

Interior Low Plateaus
Highland Rim Section
Blind valleys (valley sinks)
Caves (Mammoth Cave, etc.)
Cuesta (Dripping Springs Cuesta)
Dissected plateau
Entrenched meander (Turnhole Bend)
Entrenched stream
Karst topography (on dissected plateau, north portion of map; and on lowland, near base level of subterranean streams, south portion of map)
Sink (Hunts Sink, Cedar Sink)
Slip-off slopes (Green River)
Springs (Dripping Springs)
Undercut slopes (Green River)

LOUISIANA

Campti, 42

West Gulf Coastal Plain
Bed of drained shallow lake (Old Spanish Lowlands)
Cut-bank
Flood plain (Red River)
Flood plain swamps
Marsh or swamp
Meandering stream (Red River)
Natural levee
Oxbow lake
River shore bars
Sloughs (Bayou Pierre, etc.)

South Pass, 43

Coastal Plain—Mississippi Alluvial Plain
Deltaic channel
Inactive distributaries

MAINE

Katahdin, 44

New England Province
White Mountain Section
Arête (Knife Edge)
Biscuit-board topography
Cirque
Col
Cyclopean stairs
Glacial drift
Hanging valley (North Basin, etc.)
Kames
Meanders (Sandy Stream)
Monadnock (Mount Katahdin, said to be the first point on which morning sun shines on continental United States)
Marsh or swamp
Ponds in kettles
Radial drainage (Mount Katahdin)
Strongly dissected mountainous highland
Tarn
Waterfall or rapids

Mount Desert, 45

New England Province
Seaboard Lowland Section
Bay
Cliff
Cove
Drowned coast line
Fiord (Somes Sound)
Finger lakes
Lakes and ponds in glacially scoured bedrock basins
Mountains and islands modified by continental glaciation
Narrows
Rock sculpture controlled by fractures (Seal Cove Pond, etc.)
Tidal marsh

MARYLAND/WEST VIRGINIA

Cumberland, 46

Valley and Ridge Province
Middle Section (also portion of Appalachian Plateau)
Allegheny Front
Anticlinal ridge (Wills Mountain)
Gorge (The Narrows)
Stream piracy (lower course Braddock Run diverted by tributary of Wills Creek)
Structurally controlled drainage

Superposed stream, cutting water gap
in anticlinal ridge at The Narrows
Water gaps, The Narrows and at
Courthouse)

MASSACHUSETTS

Ayer, 47

New England Province
New England Upland and Seaboard
Lowland Sections
Drumlins
Esker
Glacial swamps
Kame plains
Kame terrace
Linear ridge controlled by bedrock
structure (Oak Hill)
Marsh or swamp
Ponds in kettles

Lynn, 48

New England Province
Seaboard Lowland Section
Artificial land
Ponds in glacially scoured bedrock
basins
Tidal marsh or swamp
Tombolo (complex) at Nahant

Provincetown, 49

New England Province
Seaboard Lowland Section
Beach
Compound recurved spit, prograding
(Cape Cod)
Harbor
Lagoon
Ponds in depressions
Sand dunes
Spits (Long Point)
Tidal swamp

MICHIGAN

Delaware, 50

Superior Upland
Cuesta
Dip slope along north portions
Esker
Glacial drift (faint)
Hogback (north portion of map)
Immature drainage (throughout map)
Ridge and valley topography (north
and central portions of map)
Swamp or bog
Water Gap
Wind Gap at elevation 1065

Fennville, 51

Central Lowlands—Eastern Lake Section
Abandoned river mouths
Blowout dune
Cutoff meanders (in Kalamazoo River)
Drainage canals
Entrenched tributaries
(Roelofs Gulley, etc.)
Intermorainal lowland
Knobs and kettles

Lakeshore dunes
(east shore Lake Michigan)
Morainic topography (Lake Border,
west portion, and Valparaiso, east
portion)
Pitted outwash plain
Raised beach ridges
Raised spit and hook (at Douglas)
River terrace
Sand dunes, modern active dunes at
lake shore
Swamps
Wave-cut cliffs

Jackson, 52

Central Lowland—Eastern Lake Section
Abandoned glacial channels
Artificial drainage (Grand River)
Esker (Blue Ridge)
Kames
Knobs and kettles
Lake in kettle, etc.
Morainic topography, terminal
(Kalamazoo Moraine—south portion
of map)
Pitted outwash plain
Ponds in kettles
Poorly integrated drainage with
many lakes
Swamp or marsh
Till plain (north portion of map)

MINNESOTA
(See also Wisconsin/Minnesota, Alma)

Virginia, 53

Superior Upland
Glacially rounded hills
Linear ridge of crystalline
rocks (Laurentian Divide)
Mine dumps, tailings and tailings
ponds
Monadnock
Morainic topography
Swamp or bog
Wind gap

MISSISSIPPI

Phillipp, 54

Coastal Plain
Mississippi Alluvial Plain
Ancient river bluff (partially dissected)
Abandoned channels
Cutoff meander (Tippo Bayou)
Flood plain swamp
Marsh or swamp
Meander patterns (large and small)
Meander scars
Meandering stream on alluvial plain
(Tippo Bayou)
Mississippi alluvial plain
(known as "The Delta")
Oxbow lakes
Oxbow swamp

MISSOURI
Camden, 55
Central Lowlands—Dissected Till Plains
Abandoned channels

Artificial levee
Coal mines
Dissected plains
Flood plain of Missouri River
Meander scars
River bluff
Sand bars and scrolls
Swamp areas

Ironton, 56

Ozark Plateaus—Springfield-Salem
Plateaus—Saint Francis Mountains
Region
Apex of Ozark Plateau
Centripetal drainage (all drains
originate within boundaries of this
quadrangle)
Dissected upland (known as the Iron
Mountain Country)
Knob, not glaciated

MONTANA

Chief Mountain, 57

Northern Rocky Mountains
Alpine topography
Arête
Cirque
Cirque lake
Col
Continental Divide
Cyclopean stairs
Erosion surfaces, mature type
(Flattop Mountain and Granite Park)
Finger Lakes
Glacial trough
Glacier
Glacier wall (cliff surface)
Hanging valley
Klippe (Chief Mountain)
Matterhorn
Mountain ranges (Lewis Range, etc.)
Pass (Logan Pass)
Stream piracy (Kipp Creek beheaded
branch of Waterton River)
Tarn
U-shaped valley
Wind gap (Kootenai Pass)

Ennis, 58

Northern Rocky Mountains
Alluvial fan
Alpine topography
Braided stream (Madison River)
Canyon
Cirque
Coalescing alluvial fans
Flood plain of Madison River
Glaciated valleys
Parallel drainage
Radial drainage
Terrace, alluvial

NEBRASKA

Ashby, 59

Great Plains Province
Sand Hills of Nebraska
(in High Plains Section)
Concave slope, exemplary of leeside

NEBRASKA

Ashby, 59 *(continued)*

Depression with lake
Dune topography
High water table with lakes, marshes, and flowing wells
Large scale dune ridges (some transverse) modified by secondary wind erosion, following stabilization (numerous minor blowouts)
Nonintegrated drainage

NEVADA

Sonoma Range, 60

Basin and Range Province
Great Basin Section
Bajadas (throughout map)
Bolson
Dissected block mountains
Fault scarp
Flat
Gap or pass (numerous)
Playa
Volcanic cones (one occupied by Airway Beacon east of Buffalo Valley)

NEW HAMPSHIRE

Crawford Notch, 61

New England Province
White Mountain Section
Bedrock knobs
Cascades
Cirque
Cliff
Dissected mountains of crystalline rocks overridden by glaciers
Falls
Hanging valley
Notch (Carrigan Notch)
Presidential Range of White Mountains
Ponds heading drainage (Shoal Pond, head of Shoal Pond Brook, Norcross Pond, head of Norcross Brook, etc.)
Ridge (Signal Ridge, Bemis Ridge, etc.)
Tarn
U-shaped valley (Saco River)

Monadnock, 62

New England Upland
Bedrock hills in crystalline rocks, abraded by glaciation
Concave slopes (Monadnock Mountain)
Drainage deranged by continental glaciation
Glacial drift
Hanging valleys
Kame terraces
Kettle holes
Lakes in kettle holes
Monadnock Mountain (feature from which Davis derived physiographic term)
Morainal lakes
Mountain peak (isolated)

NEW MEXICO

Bottomless Lakes, 64

Great Plains Province
Pecos Valley Section
Braided stream pattern (Pecos River)
Erosional remnant
Escarpment
Lakes in sinks, caused by solution and removal of gypsum (Bottomless Lakes)
Marsh or swamp in river bottom
Meandering stream (Pecos River)
Oxbow lake
Sink holes on dissected plain

Ship Rock, 65

Colorado Plateaus—Navajo Section
Dikes (radial)
Dip slopes
Gully, deeply eroded (Little Ship Rock Wash)
Hogback
Volcanic necks (Ship Rock, also Mitten Rock)

NEW JERSEY

Paterson, 63

New England Upland and Northern Piedmont Lowland (Triassic Lowland)
Glacially modified hills
Ice-contact slope (northeast of Preakness School, across pond 281)
Kame terraces
Kettles
Lakes in kettles (Franklin Lake, etc.)
Marsh or swamp
Meltwater channel (along Preakness Brook)
Structurally controlled drainage
Swales (between ridges)
Watchung Mountains (formed on tilted diabase sheets)

NEW YORK

Amsterdam, 66

Appalachian Plateaus—Mohawk Section
Deranged drainage, glacial (north)
Dissected glaciated plateau (southern part of map)
Glacial gorges or spillways (Wolf Hollow, etc.)
Kames (northeast of Marraville Lake)
Linear drumloidal topography
Old Erie Canal (abandoned)
River bluffs (Mohawk River)
Terraced sand plain (south of radio station)
Topographic grain, glacially modified (southeast portion of map)
U-shaped valley with terraced banks (Mohawk River Valley)

Catskill, 67

Valley and Ridge Province

Hudson Valley Section
Cliffs (west side of map)
Delta (Saugerties)
Dendritic drainage pattern
Dissected glaciated plateau bounded on east by escarpment (west portion of map)
Drowned river (Hudson River)
Drumlins (Cross Hill, Round Top and Whaleback, etc.)
Elongate folds and ice-carved strike ridges (west portion of map)
Limestone quarries
Narrow ridges
Reverse drainage (Esopus Creek, etc.)
Sand plain, glacial
Stream in narrow rock gorge (Esopus Creek)
Strike valley (Beaver Kill and Kaaterskill Creek)
Topographic grain accentuated by glacial scour (throughout map)
Water gap (High Falls)

Ithaca West, 68

Appalachian Plateaus—Southern New York Section—Finger Lakes Region
Convex slopes
Delta
Drainage at right angles to glacial trough
Southern New York section Appalatian Plateau with 1,100 feet relief on this map
Stream in glacial trough

Ticonderoga, 69

Adirondack Province (also Champlain Section of Saint Lawrence Province)
Adirondack Mountains (east boundary)
Cuesta
Dip slope
Fault block mountains (second cycle)
Post glacial lake
Structurally controlled valleys and mountains

NORTH CAROLINA

Mount Mitchell, 70

Blue Ridge Province
Southern Section (also portion of Piedmont Upland)
Blue Ridge Front (southeast portion of map)
Complexly dissected mountainous highland
Dendritic drainage (weak structural control)
Erosional escarpment (Blue Ridge Front)
Highest point in Eastern United States (Mount Mitchell)
Knobs not glaciated
Subcontinental Divide (Blue Ridge) between Gulf and Atlantic drainages
Wind Gap (Swannanoa Gap)

Index to physiographic features by feature

In this index, individual features and the maps on which they appear are listed alphabetically under 12 general headings or types of physiographic features. The 12 general headings are:

Coastal Features and Shorelines

Escarpment Features

Glaciation Features (Alpine)

Glaciation Features (Continental)

Miscellaneous Features

Mountain Features

Plains Features

Solution Features

Valley Features

Volcanic Features

Water Features

Wind Features

COASTAL FEATURES AND SHORELINES

ESCARPMENT FEATURES (cliffs, cuestas, hogbacks, etc.)

GLACIATION FEATURES FORMED BY ALPINE GLACIATION

GLACIATION FEATURES RESULTING FROM CONTINENTAL GLACIATION

MISCELLANEOUS FEATURES

MOUNTAIN FEATURES *(ridges, hills, faults, folds, etc.)*

PLAINS FEATURES

PLATEAU FEATURES *(buttes, mesas, outliers, etc.)*

SOLUTION FEATURES

VALLEY FEATURES *(basins, channels, drainage patterns, fans, meanders, terraces, etc.)*

VOLCANIC FEATURES

Ancient Mount Mazama
Crater Lake National Park, Ore., 79

Caldera
Crater Lake National Park, Ore., 79

Cinder cones
Bray, Calif., 17
Menan Buttes, Idaho, 33

Collapse depressions
Bray, Calif., 17

Collapsed volcanic cone
Crater Lake National Park, Ore., 79

Crater
Crater Lake National Park, Ore., 79

Menan Buttes, Idaho, 33

Dikes, radial
Ship Rock, N. M., 65

Dissected volcano
Crater Lake National Park, Ore., 79

Eroded volcanic mountains
Bray, Calif., 17

Faulted volcanic cone
Chemult, Ore., 78

Nuees ardentes deposits
Crater Lake National Park, Ore., 79

Parasitic cone
Crater Lake National Park, Ore., 79

Radial drainage on volcanic cone
Mount Rainier, Wash., 104

Recent vulcanism
Chemult, Ore., 78

Rim of caldera
Crater Lake National Park, Ore., 79

Shield volcano
Crater Lake National Park, Ore., 79

Stripped lava flow surface
Yakima East, Wash., 105

Volcanic cone
Chemult, Ore., 78
Mount Rainier, Wash., 104

Volcanic cone, breached
Crater Lake National Park, Ore., 79

Volcanic cone within caldera
Crater Lake National Park, Ore., 79

Volcanic necks and plugs
Santiago Peak, Texas, 93
Ship Rock, N. M., 65

Volcanic tableland
Mount Tom, Calif., 19

Water gap in lava
Yakima East, Wash., 105

WATER FEATURES *(lakes, streams, etc.)*

Abandoned channels
(see VALLEY FEATURES)

Abandoned river mouths
Fennville, Mich., 51

Antecedent stream
Yakima East, Wash., 105

Artificial drainage
Jackson, Mich., 52

Bayou
(see COASTAL FEATURES)

Braided stream
Bottomless Lakes, N. M., 64
Ennis, Mont., 58

Consequent streams
Yakima East, Wash., 105

Cutoff meanders
Fennville, Mich., 51
Philipp, Miss., 54

Deep lakes in solution basins
Bottomless Lakes, N. M., 64
Lakes Wales, Fla., 31

Disappearing stream
Oolitic, Ind., 36
Rover, Tenn., 89

Finger lake
(see GLACIATION FEATURES, CONTINENTAL)

High water table
Ashby, Neb., 59

Kettle with lake
(see GLACIATION FEATURES, CONTINENTAL)

Lake dammed by landslide
Marysvale, Utah, 97

Lakes in sinks
(see SOLUTION FEATURES)

Marshy divide
Ithaca West, N. Y., 68

Mineral springs
Furnace Creek, Calif., 18

Morainal lakes
(see GLACIATION FEATURES, CONTINENTAL)

Oxbows
Voltaire, N. D., 74

Oxbow lake
Campti, La., 42
East Brownsville, Texas, 91
Marysville, Utah, 97

Oxbow swamp
Philipp, Miss., 54

Ponds in kettles
(see GLACIATION FEATURES, CONTINENTAL)

Ponds heading drainage
Crawford Notch, N. H., 61

Poorly integrated drainage
(see GLACIATION FEATURES, CONTINENTAL)

Post-glacial lake in drowned valley
Ticonderoga, N. Y., 69

Rapids
Maumee, Ohio, 75
Thousand Springs, Idaho, 34

River with sand channel
(see VALLEY FEATURES)

Shallow lakes on coastal terrace
Lake Wales, Fla., 31

Slough
Campti, La., 42
Menan Buttes, Idaho, 33

Springs
Crater Lake National Park, Ore., 79
Thousand Springs, Idaho, 34

Stream piracy
(see VALLEY FEATURES)

Subsequent stream
Yakima East, Wash., 105

Superposed stream
Cumberland, Md./W. Va., 46
Warm Springs, Ga., 32

Waterfall
Ithaca West, N. Y., 68

Water gap
(see MOUNTAIN FEATURES

Waterholes
Turkey Mountain, Texas, 94

WIND FEATURES

Blowout dune
Fennville, Mich., 51

Clay dune
East Brownsville, Texas, 91

Deflation basins
Bottomless Lakes, N. M., 64
Lake McBride, Kan., 38

Dune ridges, some transverse
Ashby Neb., 59

Dunes and beach ridges
Jacksonville Beach, Fla., 30

Dunes and deation hollows
Sheep Mountain Table, S. D., 87

Dune topography
Ashby, Neb., 59

Lakeshore dunes
Fennville, Mich., 51

Large scale dune ridges
Ashby, Neb., 59

Sand bars and scrolls
(see VALLEY FEATURES)
Sand dunes
Commerce City, Colo., 24
Fennville, Mich., 51
Provincetown, Mass., 49
Sand hills
Ashby, Neb., 59